Mysteries of *Dune*

Also from
Temple of Justice Books

Alchemy in Middle-earth:
The Significance of J.R.R. Tolkien's
The Lord of the Rings

The Red and the White:
Perspectives on America and the
Primordial Tradition

Mahmoud Shelton

Mysteries of *Dune*

Sufism, Psychedelics,
and the Prediction of
Frank Herbert

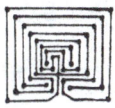

Temple of Justice Books

In memory of my father
Dr. Jack Shelton

Second Edition
Copyright © 2020 D.M. Shelton

All rights reserved. This book or any portion thereof may
not be reproduced or used in any manner whatsoever
without the express written permission of the publisher.

Temple of Justice Books
templeofjustice@icloud.com

Printed in the United States of America
by Lightning Source Inc.

ISBN 978-0-9741468-2-9

Cover photographs
Front: At the Oregon Dunes
Back: Cavern in the San Francisco Bay Area

Contents

1	Some Enigmas	7
2	Alam al-mithal	14
3	Doors in the Wall	22
4	Lisan al-gaib	30
5	Sun of Atreus	36
6	Buddislam?	43
7	Shai-hulud	53
8	Usul	59
9	Golden Gate	67

Mountaineer of the Caucasus
The artist Prince Gagarin presents his subject adorned with *kindjal* dagger and *bourka* mantle that both belong likewise to *Dune*

1

Some Enigmas

As a literary genre, science fiction plays with prophecy. Instead of delivering messages from Heaven to benefit life on Earth, the writers of science fiction derive their speculations from the state of things on the earth, even while their vision seems preoccupied with locations in space, or rather in the heavens. Since these speculations look forward, the genre has always included predictions that sometimes seem prophetic in hindsight. No work of this genre embodies the concern with prophecy so apparently as *Dune* by Frank Herbert, since it explicitly concerns the rise of a religious prophet. As if to reinforce the importance of this relationship between science fiction and prophecy, *Dune* is also held to be the best-selling work of the genre.

The primary inspiration for *Dune* is traced to author Frank Herbert's research into the American government's efforts to control the ecology of the Oregon Dunes along his native West Coast; and although it was never completed, the report of this research, entitled "They Stopped the Shifting Sands," would lead to the global ecological concerns of *Dune*. According to the biography written by his son, Herbert was affected by the American Indian worldview belonging to his closest friend, Herbie Hansen of the Quileute tribe, who insisted: "The Earth is dying, it is being misused by non-Indian civilizations that take and do not give." Moreover, given the importance of religion in *Dune*, it should be pointed out that Herbert and his friend "drew parallels between Zen Buddhism, Hinduism, the

Kabbalah of Judaism, the Sufis of Islam, and Native American beliefs."

The first appendices of Herbert's novel are concerning "The Ecology of Dune" and "The Religion of Dune," respectively. Regarding the former, and with reference to his father's upbringing in Washington state, Brian Herbert claims: "The increasing pollution he saw all around him, in the city of his birth, contributed to his resolve that something had to be done to save the Earth. This became, perhaps, the most important message of *Dune*."[1] The principal resource of the imaginary planet "Dune" or Arrakis is a substance called spice, to be considered in due course; but since Arrakis is a desert planet, it may be easily understood that the ecological concerns of Dune focus on the scarcity of water. This particular emphasis is unrelated to any research on the Oregon Dunes, and yet it does accord with contemporary Native American beliefs. The late Agnes Baker Pilgrim, a Native elder from Oregon whose influence was felt worldwide, understood her role in the 21st century to be as a defender of water especially, and that a coming conflict would be rooted in its misuse.

As far as religion is concerned, there is no doubt that for its depiction in an imaginary distant future, Herbert relied first and foremost upon the religion of Islam, despite the syncretic addition of prefixes in his names for it, such as "Zensunni," or even "Buddislam." Perhaps his discussions on comparative religion led him to recognize Islam's unique identification with the Primordial Tradition; more likely he could most easily imagine the preservation of Islam into a distant future. Be that as it may, even a cursory glance at the appended "Glossary of the Imperium" in *Dune* reveals not

---

[1] Several quotations from *Dreamer of Dune*, New York: Tor, 2003, pages 146-7.

Some Enigmas

merely the preponderance of Arabic words,[2] but that the meanings of these real words are often enough relatively unchanged: to provide just a few examples, fiqh is "religious law" and ulema is a "doctor of theology" (the Arabic word `ulama is actually the plural form of `alim), and the month of Ramadhan is still the ninth month dedicated to religious fasting. In keeping with this relative adherence to traditional lore,[3] an imagined future revitalization of religion must in Islamic terms involve the apocalyptic leader known as the Mahdi, and this is precisely the title of the prophesied leader of *Dune*.

Despite the litany of languages and religious influences that Herbert's son offers in a recent afterword to the novel, it is disingenuous – or ignorant - to downplay the role given to Islam and its sacred language in *Dune*. With the Bible being the only traditional reference for modern Westerners, the understanding of Islam and its Arab foundation must derive from the account in Genesis of the exile of Ishmael with his mother (who is a concubine) in the desert; and such is indeed the plight of Paul and his mother in *Dune*.[4] Of course, this literal reliance reduces the

---

[2] The same may not be claimed for any language that has been employed as a vehicle for Buddhism, such as Japanese.

[3] Fuller traces of traditional lore may in fact be found: a Tradition (*hadith*) of the Prophet Muhammad, "Haste is from Shaitan," becomes in *Dune*, "Speed comes from Shaitan," with the Arabic name for "Satan" maintained. Herbert later would quote Qur'an XXXVI, 9 verbatim as an example of that which is "written in the old Fremen religion" (*Children of Dune*, New York: ACE, 2008, page 9).

[4] Just as the Biblical Ishmael recalls Islam for Westerners, so is the name Paul synonymous with Christianity. There is a Tradition in Islam affirming that "There is no Mahdi if not Jesus," which should not be understood to deny the unique identity of the former that will be of great importance to our subject, but rather to indicate the essential function of the Mahdi as preparing the world for Jesus' apocalyptic return. Herbert's choice of the name Paul for his Mahdi indicates this attachment to Jesus, despite the disdain

originality of the author's vision, something his son has no interest in belittling, to say the least; but given the finality of the Islamic revelation, the reliance upon the eschatology of Islam in particular is, in fact, appropriate for a "dying" Earth.[5]

The subject of Herbert's sources has been illuminated by a recent article published in the *Los Angeles Review of Books*, "The Secret History of Dune" by Will Collins. Here the author establishes that a primary source for Herbert was the book *The Sabres of Paradise* by Lesley Blanch, an account of the Murid Wars of the mid-19th century. Although Collins considers this source "idiosyncratic," it should rather be admitted that it is consistent with Herbert's awareness of the "Sufis of Islam," since the Murids who resisted Russian Imperialism in the Caucasus were followers of the Naqshbandi order of Sufism. The article is no doubt helpful in establishing that Herbert mined themes, more terminology, and even particular passages from this account of Naqshbandi history.

Unfortunately, the article is less discriminating when it comes to another matter of particular importance: "Even a casual political observer will recognize the parallels between the universe of *Dune* and the Middle East of the late 20th century. Islamic theology, mysticism, and the history of the Arab world clearly influenced *Dune*..." Here Collins apparently has in mind the parallel between Iraq and the proper name of the planet Dune, Arrakis, with oil corresponding to the precious Spice. No doubt this association is reinforced by Herbert's inclusion of the name Habbanya, a place in Iraq, in Arrakis' geography. It is also

---

for the historical Paul that prevails in the Muslim world; but Herbert, of course, did not belong to that world.
[5] On the identification of Islam with the Primordial Tradition, as well as the link between Islamic eschatology and the American Indian view of environmental renewal, see *The Red and the White*.

clear that the name of the "Padishah" holding power over Arrakis, Emperor Shaddam, recalls the tyrant Saddam Hussein. However, it is extremely unlikely that Herbert had this last association in mind, since Saddam Hussein was an exiled minor figure in Iraqi affairs when Herbert was composing *Dune*; yet this enigma is all too often passed over, as it has been here.

Collins continues: "...the Murids' austerely militant Islamic faith recalls the theology of modern fundamentalists." This statement is dangerously irresponsible. Even a "casual" observer of theology must recognize that modern fundamentalists, or Wahhabis, follow a "reformed" Islam with a new *fiqh* (to use the relevant term); and that, on the contrary, the Naqshbandi spirituality and military resistance of the Murids proceeded from their fulfilment of traditional Islamic law. Moreover, the Sufis are focused on the inner jihad of the soul, and so understand the jihad of the battlefield only as an outward and hence secondary application. Another fact that a casual observer will recognize is that the favorite targets of the terrorism that proceeds from Wahhabism are none other than Islam's sacred shrines and the Sufis who frequent them, since Wahhabism utterly rejects the esoterism of Islam. Now, it must be admitted that the career of T. E. Lawrence has been cited among the inspirations for Herbert's work, and that Lawrence supported the Wahhabi revolt in Arabia. Nevertheless, a more careful consideration of the terminology of *Dune* will discover an abundance of terms and concepts belonging only to the doctrines of Sufism, or rather Islamic esoterism. This emphasis on Sufism, traceable both in his personal experience and through the irrefutable inspiration of the Murid Wars, stands in precise opposition to "modern fundamentalists."

These clarifications are essential in order to properly consider two interrelated enigmas that have arisen since the original publication of *Dune*. First of all, despite the novel's depiction of how a religious prophecy came to be unquestionably fulfilled,[6] Herbert would eventually follow up his work with sequels supposing that this fulfillment was somehow false. The rise of the native Fremen in *Dune* brings the overthrow of those who "take and do not give," recalling Herbert's sympathy with the American Indian perspective; yet following the victory of this worldview in his novel, and in spite of the promise of transforming an ecological wasteland, Herbert chose to undermine his victory. Even John W. Campbell, one of Herbert's greatest supporters who served as the work's first publisher, refused to publish its sequel because of Herbert's about-face concerning the hero of the story.[7] No matter what Herbert's reasoning, this decision by the author has only recently assumed a striking relevance, due to a second development.

This development, that followed Herbert's writing by nearly half a century, is the rise of the so-called "Islamic State" in Iraq. It is not merely the location that specifically resonates with *Dune*, nor the religious posturing of the movement that emerged in an ongoing struggle over oil;[8] and even while acknowledging that the emergence of the movement coincided with the fall of Saddam, like the

---

[6] For this reason, the fulfilment of the Zensunni prophecies may be compared neither to the frustrated hopes of Shi`ism, nor with the Sudanese revolt of the Sufi pretender to the rank of al-Mahdi, since neither fulfilled the prophecies of orthodox or Sunni Islam.

[7] "Unpublished Interview with Frank Herbert and Professor Willis E. McNelly," 3 February 1969, retrieved 22 November 2019 via sinanvural.com

[8] It may also be observed that the leader of House Harkonnen is named Vladimir, and while this name evokes the Russian adversaries in the Murid Wars, it also happens to be the name of the contemporary Russian leader. Taking this still further, the rival House Atreides' home planet of Caladan even recalls the New World character Caliban from the works of Shakespeare that are certainly to be included among Herbert's sources, and this serves well enough to suggest the American origin of Russia's rival in the Middle East.

Some Enigmas

ousting of the Padishah on Arrakis, it is above all in the eschatological propaganda of ISIS[9] that the movement recalls the plot of *Dune* so precisely. It is essential to properly identify ISIS as a development of Wahhabism, indeed as its most extreme, since its audacity extended not only to indiscriminate bloodshed in a false jihad but also to the establishment of a pretend caliphate, in keeping with its eschatological pose. For now, it is enough to recognize that it was in particular the abuse of jihad that Herbert employed in the *Dune* series to denigrate the apparent victory in his original story.

This confusion, proceeding from Herbert's mining of the Islamic tradition for his account that has come to reflect so startlingly developments concerning anti-traditional Islam, provides, in fact, a remarkable example of the spirit of the times. That Herbert understood something of the import of his work in space and time is suggested in the special dedication that he would offer at the opening of *Dune*:

> To the people whose labors go beyond ideas into the realm of "real materials" – to the dry-land ecologists, wherever they may be, in whatever time they work, *this effort at prediction* is dedicated in humility and admiration.[10]

---

[9] It should not be overlooked that the acronym ISIS (for "Islamic State of Iraq and Syria") evokes the ancient Egyptian goddess who has become a patron of sorts in contemporary witchcraft, and that the Fremen uprising on Dune depended upon the machinations of the Bene Gesserit "witches" very intimately.

[10] Italics added for emphasis. More than once it has been claimed that "the function of science fiction is not only to predict the future but to prevent it." Although these words have been attributed to Herbert (Timothy O'Reilly, *Frank Herbert*, New York: Ungar, 1981, page 14), Ray Bradbury is more often remembered as the originator of this quote.

2

Alam al-mithal

Concerning Herbert's sources, both apparent and hidden, there is an important key to be discovered among the many Arabic terms he adapted for his work. The relatively obscure term "alam al-mithal" belongs exclusively to the language of Islamic esoterism, and its presence in the pages of *Dune* betrays another specific source for Herbert. This source is the prolific work of the orientalist Henri Corbin, whose focus on the `alam ul-mithal resulted in *L'imagination créatrice dans le soufisme d'Ibn 'Arabi*[1] published in 1958; in fact, its contents were first published two years before that, in proceedings of the Eranos Conference in Switzerland. This detail is not irrelevant, since Carl Jung was likewise a participant in Eranos, and it is well known that Herbert was influenced by his psychology through friendship with one of Jung's students, Irene Slattery. As for Corbin's studies on Islamic esoterism, Herbert could even have discovered there the

---

[1] Corbin's study focuses on the personality of the Greatest Master of Islamic esoterism, Ibn `Arabi. It should be noted that Shaykh Muhyiddin Ibn `Arabi is not generally considered to be the founder of an order, but his legacy instead became attached to the Naqshbandi order specifically, that is, to the very order with which Herbert was familiar through the account of the Murid Wars (Cf. Michel Chodkiewicz, *The Spiritual Writings of Amir `Abd al-Kader*, Albany: SUNY, 1995, page 20).

term *kathib* for a posthumous location of Divine disclosure, a term translated simply as "dune."[2]

In addition to its exposition in the narrative, Herbert provides a definition for alam al-mithal in his Glossary of the Imperium: "the mystical world of similitudes where all physical limitations are removed." In his second appendix, "The Religion of Dune," he explains further that this world is "the land of the ruh-spirit." Despite the fact that `alam ul-mithal* has indeed been translated from the Arabic as "World of Similitudes," and that "ruh" does mean spirit, a point which Herbert reinforces by his conjunction "ruh-spirit," the identification of the alam al-mithal as the domain of the ruh is technically incorrect. Islamic esoterism identifies the `alam ul-mithal* as being positioned between two other worlds, the `alam ul-ajsam* or "World of Bodies" and the `alam ul-arwah* or "World of Spirits;" for this reason it is also called the `alam ul-barzakh,* literally the "World of the In-between." Despite the insufficiencies of English terminology, the soul or psyche (*nafs*) may be said to be between the spirit and the body. Now this distinction is not merely academic; unlike the pure World of Spirits, the `alam al-mithal* is the domain of psychic forces beneficent or harmful. *Mithal* means images, and the imaginative faculty of the soul is known as *wahm* in Arabic, a word that signifies among other things "deceit" or "illusion."

That Herbert should have confused the Worlds of Images and of Spirits is not too surprising, despite his apparent reliance upon traditional sources. Cartesian dualism had long before replaced for Westerners the traditional understanding of the three worlds of the human being. As a consequence, Jungian psychology perceives beyond the physical only the obscurity of an "unconscious," despite references to "archetypes" that, if properly

---

[2] *Spiritual Body and Celestial Earth,* translated by Nancy Pearson, Princeton: Princeton University Press, 1977, page 150.

understood, should be assigned a higher source. The confusion of the psychic and spiritual is addressed by René Guénon in *The Reign of Quantity and the Signs of the Times*.[3] In this urgently important work, he also refers to a cosmic wall that separates the corporeal realm from the psychic world immediately "outside" it, as well as the weakening of that barrier from the stages of anti-traditional action. In Islamic sources, this barrier is known as the Wall of Alexander that was constructed between "twin peaks" by Alexander the Great,[4] protecting the physical world from the destructive forces of Gog and Magog who are expected to break through it at the End of Time. The weakening of this barrier is in fact indicated in a Tradition of the Prophet of Islam concerning a *"danger that has come near:"*

> *"...An opening has been made in the Wall of Gog and Magog like this," making a circle with his thumb and index finger. Zaynab bint Jahsh said, "O Messenger of Allah, shall we be destroyed even though there are pious people among us? He said, "Yes, when the evil people will increase."*[5]

René Guénon, who is also known by the initiatory name Shaykh Abd al-Wahid Yahya, reminds us that the nature of a wall is to act "both as a protection and as a

---

[3] Translated from the French by Lord Northbourne, Baltimore: Penguin Books, 1972 (first published in English in 1953).

[4] Qur'an XVIII, 92-98. Folklore situates the geographic location of this barrier, curiously enough, in the Caucasus mountains in general and Daghestan in particular. This association is mentioned, though not correctly understood, by Blanch in *The Sabres of Paradise*.

[5] *Sahih Bukhari*. The emphasis on building a border wall in American politics serves to parody the importance of ensuring the stability of this cosmic wall. Not only is it a distraction, but it is accomplished in violation of ecological and indigenous justice.

Alam al-mithal

limitation," and therefore has "both advantages and inconveniences;"[6] and so we may clearly understand the relationship between morality – at times "limiting" and "inconvenient" - and this barrier, since in both cases dangerous psychic forces are being kept out; and this correspondence is in keeping with the identity of the human being as microcosm. In all that follows, it is important to keep the relationship between the human microcosm and the macrocosm in mind.

To provide another example relevant to Frank Herbert, the doctrine of the three worlds is also formulated in the American Indian cosmology of Sky World, Underworld, and Earth. It may therefore be understood that the psychic realm immediately beyond this world of bodies may also be understood as located "under" or below. As an echo of the cosmic wall described above, it should be recognized that the ubiquitous stone walls of the American landscape – whether passed over as farmers' walls in New England or more perceptively termed "Mystery Walls" in the West - traditionally served to separate the Earth from unseen dangers; for this reason, such a wall was employed for protection by a Shawnee medicine man confronting a horned serpent of the Underworld.[7] What is more, many traditional examples might be offered that express correspondences with the three worlds. For example, in the sacred syllable Om, or more exactly Aum, each Sanskrit letter represents one of the three states of wakefulness,

---

[6] Op. cit., page 205.

[7] Loubser and Frink, "An Archaeological and Ethnohistorical Appraisal of a Piled Stone Feature Complex in the Mountains of North Georgia," *Early Georgia*, volume 38, number 1, page 32. This reference is unusual, however, since the very existence of these stone monuments has been chronically ignored by modern archaeologists. Their failure is easily accounted for, however, since materialistic science is prevented from recognizing a purpose relating to a realm that it pretends doesn't exist; yet this failure also fails to ensure their preservation.

dreaming, and deep sleep;[8] and so references to a "waking dream" in *Dune* may be understood to indicate an intrusion of the psychic world into the corporeal.

To properly understand the psychic realm is the reason for the presence of subterranean mysteries in mythology and ancient ritual, and so the initiatory cavern is not only present but even predominates in the Islamic tradition. For example, during the flight from Mecca to Yathrib, the Prophet Muhammad and his best friend Abu Bakr as-Siddiq took refuge from pursuing forces in a cave.[9] Their location was further hidden by the miraculous arrival of a pair of doves who took up positions at the cavern entrance. According to traditional sources,[10] the cavern was the home of a poisonous serpent, who had made innumerable holes in the interior of the cave. During their rest, Abu Bakr blocked a hole with his body through which the serpent hoped to glimpse the beauty of the Prophet,[11] and so he was bitten. Having removed the poison from his friend's foot, the Prophet forgave and blessed the serpent, rendering it and its progeny harmless ever after. This cave is remembered in Naqshbandi sources as the place where

---

[8] See Michel Valsan, "Le Triangle de l'Androgyne et la Monosyllable Om" in *L'Islam et la Fonction de René Guénon*, Paris: Les Editions de l'Oeuvre, 1984.

[9] The name of this cave – *Thawr* or "bull" – recalls the subterranean container for the Minotaur, the labyrinth. The inclusion of a labyrinth in a Gothic cathedral suggests that its builders understood its symbolism, according to which the successful passage of the labyrinth grants access to spiritual rewards. What is more, the labyrinth at Chartres displays the influence of Islamic esoterism, but it is hardly appropriate to elaborate on that here.

[10] Cf. Hajjah Amina Adil, *Muhammad the Last Prophet*, Washington: ISCA, 2002, page 276-8.

[11] The use of holes in stone for sight recalls the "eyed stones" of Hopi cosmology, as well as the "seven eyes" upon a stone in the Biblical Book of Zechariah (3:9).

Alam al-mithal

its initiatory chain begins, with the secret of the order passing from the Prophet to his first inheritor.

An initiatory cavern, the Cave of Birds, figures in the events of book III of *Dune*, where Paul Atreides, now known as Paul-Muad'Dib, transforms the poison of the sandworms and attains the "Water of Life." To begin with, the name of this cave, like the presence of miraculous doves, indicates a location that is open to influences of the highest order, since birds may symbolize angels who belong properly to the "World of Spirits." In a similar fashion, as we have already noted, the serpent belongs to the Underworld, or rather the `alam ul-barzakh*, and so the serpent may indeed symbolize the jinn who are considered "in-between" humans and angels in Islam.[12] Predictably, "Water of Life" (*ma' ul-hayat*) is another term belonging to Islamic esoterism, and figures as the goal of an otherworldly quest led by Alexander the Great into a Land of Darkness; appropriately, Muad'Dib is described as finding the water in "the-direction-that-is-dark." Alexander, who is identified in the Qur'an as Dhul-Qarnayn ("Lord of the Twin Horns"), is unsuccessful in his search, yet one of his companions discovers the Spring of Life; and it must be insisted that this Water appears as a spring because it rises from another world, the World of Spirits. This companion of Alexander becomes known as the immortal prophet al-Khidr, the Green Man, and it is at least partly because of his later intervention in the initiatory chain of the Naqshbandi order that an early account of this "Golden Chain" is entitled *Rashahat `ayn al-hayat* ("Droplets from the Spring of Life").

The sandworms guard the precious planetary resource known as spice or melange. Herbert confirmed that his guardian is "archetypal," like the dragon of

---

[12] On confusions between angels and *jinn*, or fairies, see chapter 4 of *The Red and the White*.

Beowulf, and properly "lives underground in the cavern."[13] Concerning such subterranean guardians, Shaykh Abd al-Wahid Yahya provides this warning:

> ...all the "legends" (using the language of to-day) about these "treasures" show clearly that their "guardians," who are none other than the subtle influences attached to them, are psychic "entities" which it is extremely dangerous for anyone to approach who has not got the required "qualifications" and does not take the necessary precautions; but what precautions could the moderns, completely ignorant of such matters, in fact be expected to take in such matters?[14]

He explains elsewhere the role of *tariqah* (what is referred to as the orders of Sufism) in allowing passage from the *shari`ah* or law to the *haqiqah* or metaphysical realization.[15] Islamic esoterism includes another term, *ma`rifah* or spiritual knowledge, and these four terms are known collectively as the Four Gateways. Each "gate" leads to the next in succession, and each has its proper authority; the *`ulama* has authority concerning the *shari'ah*,[16] for example, and the Sufi masters in *tariqah*. The abovementioned "qualifications" and "precautions" no doubt relate to an effective knowledge of these gateways.

Religion is usually understood to relate only to the first of these gateways, but it must be insisted that its

---

[13] Herbert and McNally 1969. Note that the dragon in Beowulf is called a *wyrm* or worm.

[14] Guénon 1972, page 188.

[15] *Insights into Islamic Esoterism and Taoism*, Hillsdale: Sophia Perennis, 2004, chapter 1.

[16] Mention was made earlier of Herbert's ulema, and what is more, "Shari-a" is defined rather dismissively in the Glossary of the Imperium as "superstitious ritual."

function is to provide access to further realization. The phrase "religious experience" is applied somewhat indiscriminately to all that may be reached beyond it, whereas the doctrine of the Four Gateways allows for a more penetrating understanding. The gateway of *shari`ah* may be understood to offer moral stability in the corporeal world, while that of *tariqah* provides a way to negotiate the world of the soul (*nafs*). Since the orders of Sufism are formed by means of initiatory chains of spiritual authority, these lineages must reach to the spiritual world (`*alam ul-arwah*) through the gateway of *ma`rifah*, with the Divine World reached finally through the gateway of *haqiqah*. Given the rigors of these dimensions, the peculiarly modern claim of being "spiritual but not religious" appears to belong only to the illusions of the imagination.

The Water of Life in the Land of Darkness
from the *Khamsa* of Nizami

3

Doors in the Wall

There is no room to deny that the spice or melange of Arrakis – including the Water of Life described as an "'illuminating' poison" and "`awareness spectrum' narcotic" – betrays a connection to the psychedelic drugs of the milieu in which Frank Herbert was writing, that is, the San Francisco Bay Area of the early 1960s. Not long before, the popular writer Herb Caen had dubbed San Francisco "Baghdad by the Bay," so Herbert's referencing of Iraq actually had a local literary precedent. It is known that Herbert experienced psychoactive drugs personally,[1] and it is not inconceivable that Herbert's friendly visits with Alan Watts, the influential popularizer of Zen Buddhism, included the sharing of LSD. [2] Herbert's imaginary formulation of Fremen religion is an example of the modern association of psychedelics with the religious experience; and while this subject preoccupied Watts, Aldous Huxley's *The Doors of Perception* was an earlier attempt to explore this association.

The influential title of Huxley's book is in turn drawn from William Blake's poem "The Marriage of Heaven and Hell:" "If the doors of perception were cleansed every thing would appear to man as it is: Infinite. For man has closed himself up, till he sees all things thro'

---

[1] Herbert 2003, page 184.
[2] For Herbert's friendship with Watts, see ibid., page 165. For Watts' experiences with LSD, see *The Collected Letters of Alan Watts*, Novato: New World Library, 2017, part VIII.

narrow chinks of his cavern." However, Blake's own perspective on the soul's faculty of the imagination was a departure from the traditional conception. In the descent from the spiritual to corporeal worlds, each realm is understood to be the emanation of the world immediately superior to it and upon which it depends for its existence; in this regard, there can never be an absolute separation between the three worlds. The `alam ul-mithal* may therefore provide forms for spirits, but these forms are also relatively separated from their origin, and it is through the illusion of independence that the imagination may be deceived. None other than W.B. Yeats has provided a summary of Blake's view: "He had learned from Jacob Boehme and from old alchemist writers that imagination was the first emanation of divinity, "the body of God," "the Divine members," and he drew the deduction, which they did not draw, that the imaginative arts were therefore the greatest of Divine revelations."[3] In other words, like Herbert, Blake confused the World of Spirits with the World of Images, since revelation is rather a spiritual descent directly into this world free of the illusions of the imagination. As a consequence, it is important to recognize that Blake's "doors of perception" could only access the World of Images, and not the truly infinite, for the `alam ul-mithal* is by no means beyond *all* limitations.

Huxley's title may now serve as an important indication of how we are to consider the relationship between the effects of psychedelic drugs and the religious experience. Like Blake's doors of "cleansed" perception, any physical substance that temporarily alters perception may at best only provide a glimpse into that realm lying just outside (or below) this physical world. Remarkably, a contemporary master of Naqshbandi spirituality has characterized practices in *tariqah* as specifically "*designed to break the spell of mundane consciousness, and propel the*

---

[3] "William Blake and the Imagination," 1897.

practicant into a state of altered awareness." The master Shaykh Nazim al-Haqqani, inheritor of the Daghestani chain of spiritual transmission,[4] continues:

> *Without a doubt, through the steadfast and dedicated practice of these methods the aspirant may experience spiritual states and attain stations unimaginable in a normal state of consciousness, may feel himself flying towards a heavenly goal, beholding the wonders of the mysterious and hidden aspects of creation...Through the recitation of the Most Beautiful Names of Allah everyone receives bountifully in accordance with his intention, but finally, the sincere seeker should be struck with remorse for his having pursued stations and states. One day he will perceive how he has fallen victim to distraction, and say: "Oh my Lord, I have been wasting myself and my efforts on something other than you."*[5]

No doubt there are comparisons to be made here between this description of psychic states and accounts of psychedelic experiences, but the purpose of religion aims beyond these experiences: *"You must understand that the strange and enchanting experiences are the scenery of the journey, not the goal."*[6]

The scholar of religion Huston Smith defended Huxley's *Doors of Perception* upon its publication, yet he would reach a comparable understanding concerning "religious experiences" based upon Zen Buddhism:

---

[4] "Daghestan" means literally the "Land of Mountains," and this lineage of the order was also known as Naqshbandi-Khalidi because of its inheritance from the master Khalid al-Baghdadi.
[5] *The Naqshbandi Way: A Guidebook for Spiritual Progress*, Konya: Sebat, 1982, pages 7-8.
[6] Ibid., pages 8-9.

> The case of Zen is especially pertinent here, for it pivots on an enlightenment experience – satori or kensho - which some (but not all) Zennists says resembles LSD. Alike or different, the point is that Zen recognizes that unless the experience is joined to discipline, the experience will come to naught...If the religion of religious experience is a snare and a delusion, it follows that no religion that fixes its faith primarily in substances that induce religious experiences can be expected to come to a good end. What promised to be a shortcut will prove to be a short circuit...[7]

Even in ancient times, it was recognized that there was a choice of ways to enter the underworld, as no less an authority than Plato admitted: "*I conceive that the founders of the mysteries had a real meaning and were not mere triflers when they intimated in a figure long ago that he who passes unsanctified and uninitiated into the world below will live in a slough, but that he who arrives there after initiation and purification will dwell with the gods.*"[8] *Tariqah* opens onto the world of the soul, but it is reserved for those qualified by passing first through the gateway of *shari`ah*.

In the last chapter mention was made of the cosmic wall posited between this World of Bodies and the psychic world, and also of the holes made in this wall that weaken the defense against destructive forces. Now, if psychoactive substances provide glimpses into the psychic world, their

---

[7] "Do Drugs Have Religious Import?" *The Journal of Philosophy*, 61, 18, 1964. Smith would return to the subject – and to Blake's phrase – in 2000 with *Cleansing the Doors of Perception*.

[8] *Phaedra*. "Spiritual" posturing is not equivalent to spiritual realization, even if the soul is made "happy" by it; and modern psychology's relativism concerning happiness is of no help.

use may be understood to open holes in this wall; and all too often, these substances have been instruments of irresponsibility, as in the call to "Turn on, tune in, drop out." [9] Despite dubious claims of "entheogens" being essential in ancient ritual – though perhaps they were for the "triflers," to use Plato's expression - it is surely significant that none of the religions with even a semblance of law permit their use. Even the more responsible therapeutic use of psychoactive drugs is problematic, since a doctor of psychiatry is not a proper substitute for spiritual authority. In the example of the initiatory cavern in Islam, only through the presence of the superior spiritual authority was the poison of the underworld serpent transformed; and it may be recalled that this serpent was passing through holes in the wall of that cavern.

In this regard, the use of these substances may be offered as an example of what Abd al-Wahid Yahya termed "fissures in the Great Wall" and that he warned were worsening. In the chapter of that name in *The Reign of Quantity and the Signs of the Times*, he explains that in the past, it had been the function of spiritual centers to guard against such fissures.[10] No doubt relating to this, there exists an historical account from the 9th century C.E. of the journey of Sallam the Interpreter beyond the Caucasus to the barrier against Gog and Magog, and he describes the daily vigilance of the guards at its gate.[11]

---

[9] This call was issued at the "Human Be-In" that took place, significantly enough, in Golden Gate Park in San Francisco, and inspired the "Summer of Love." "White Lightning" LSD was produced for and provided at the event.

[10] As an example of compensation for this instability, we might suggest the initiating by Shaykh Nazim al-Haqqani of unprecedented numbers of people - including Westerners new to the *shari'ah* - into the Naqshbandi way; and so he widened the gateway of *tariqah*.

[11] See Van Donzel and Schmidt, *Gog and Magog in Early Christian and Islamic Sources: Sallam's Quest for Alexander's Wall*, Leiden: Brill,

Doors in the Wall

At the barrier against Gog and Magog
from the Ottoman *Matali` us-sa`dah*

2010. The authors of this study trace Sallam's journey as far as Dunhuang in China, and this suggests that China's "Great Wall" partakes in the reality of the cosmic wall. Indeed, according to John Michell, the Great Wall of China was originally designed in accordance with Feng Shui to keep out dangerous energies. Given this understanding, it is very remarkable indeed that researchers have begun to recognize that the Great Wall of China is but a section of an even greater "wall" stretching throughout Asia, from the southern Caucasus to the Pacific Ocean, that also incorporates mountain chains (cf. Labbaf-Khaniki, M., "Long Wall of Asia: the Backbone of Asian Defensive Landscape," *Proceedings of the 10th International Congress on the Archaeology of the Ancient Near East, 25-29 April 2016, Vienna*, Wiesbaden: Harrassowitz, pages 113-20).

From this evidence, it may be seen that the locations where these fissures occur do in fact have a relationship to mundane geography. Concerning the region beyond the Wall of Alexander, there exist many depictions in Islamic miniature paintings, including the image on the previous page. Given the equivalence of serpents of the psychic realm with the sandworms of Arrakis, its subject matter bears a somewhat disconcerting resemblance to a key "image" in *Dune*, the riding of a sandworm by a multitude. At the very least, this similarity reminds us of the dangers of the `alam ul-mithal* and of the dubious inspirations that may be found there.

Similarly, the key military strategy at the novel's conclusion of employing "atomics" against the Arrakeen "Shield Wall" brings to mind nothing more than how the development of atomic weapons required the violation of the fundamental building blocks of the physical world. Neither should it be overlooked that the development of atomic power parallels the chronology of LSD's development very closely indeed. If there are tangible benefits to the therapeutic use of LSD – to break down psychic obstacles to improvement, for example – these benefits must be weighed carefully against the "waste" resulting from its use, as is indeed the case with atomic or "fission" power.

The contemporary fixation on "portals" into other dimensions – including UFO research [12] with its "Interdimensional Hypothesis" – may very well relate to the existence of fissures in the cosmic wall, even if the seekers of these potential doorways may be rather oblivious of their danger. One of the best-known examples of such a doorway

---

[12] A recent book presents evidence that UFO phenomena are focused in America upon a specific range of latitude (Ben Mezrich, *The 37th Parallel*, New York: Atria Books, 2016). It is interesting to consider that the "Long Wall of Asia" mentioned in the previous note extends along a comparable latitude, and that this alignment in America reaches to the San Francisco Bay Area.

in fiction belongs to the Narnia series by C.S. Lewis, and so it is curious that Lewis and the author of *The Doors of Perception*, Aldous Huxley, both died on the same day. The events of this date, 22 November 1963, were in fact overshadowed by the assassination of President John F. Kennedy.[13] Herbert claimed later that Kennedy embodied what he sought to warn people against in his *Dune* novels, a flawed human who dangerously assumed mythic significance.[14] Kennedy's death was thought to signal the end of the "Camelot dream;" but this thought only became established in the popular imagination later, and the earliest version of *Dune* actually appeared at exactly the same time. [15] Besides, the novel itself is rather lacking in independent evidence for Herbert's claim, so this warning may very well have been an afterthought. The timing of its first appearance, however, serves as a reminder that doorways do not only relate to space.

---

[13] The importance of this date persists in the popular imagination, as the novel *11/22/63* by Stephen King, for example, demonstrates. Concerning popular culture and this date, contemporary television coverage of the assassination in Great Britain briefly delayed the premiere episode of the series "Doctor Who;" and this show, that is still being produced more than 50 years later, concerns a "Time Lord." Perhaps it is worth noting that one of the titles of the Mahdi of Islamic eschatology is "Lord of Time" (*Sahib uz-zaman*).

[14] Herbert, "Dune Genesis," *Omni Magazine*, July 1980.

[15] This earliest version was the first installment of "Dune World" in *Analog*, and while the issue was that of December 1963, all that can be said is that the issue is likely to have been made available to newsstands right before December's arrival. Chilton Books, a company specializing in matters of industry and technical manuals, finally published the work in a single volume in 1965, the year before LSD was declared illegal in California.

4

Lisan al-gaib

If a substance from the sandworms may be compared to a psychoactive drug, there obviously can be no question of it being truly equivalent to a mystery of the spiritual realm. Frank Herbert tells a story in which a poison produces a prophet, and so he reverses the reality of the Prophet transforming a serpent's poison. The Bene Gesserit witches access a "Water of Life," but the consequence for the Fremen community is the "tau orgy" of sexual indulgence. Indeed, the Bene Gesserit are far from being recognizable as a spiritual order. The Fremen identify their practices as the "weirding way," in keeping with Shakespeare's name for the witches of Macbeth, the "weird sisters."[1] Given the Bene Gesserit obsession with political machinations, their focus is rather decidedly not on the spiritual world. Such a focus may in fact characterize the degeneration of spiritual traditions that for whatever reason have lost their way into the `alam ul-arwah, and so the inspirations for such traditions belong to the psychic realm only.

Even in the case of a living spiritual tradition, however, there exist cosmological sciences that relate to the causes of corporeal existence, and since the physical world proceeds from the psychic, these secondary sciences proceed from the `alam ul-mithal. Only when this knowledge is turned to effect changes in the corporeal

---

[1] Still, it is worth noting that the Arabic word for a practice of the soul in the orders of Sufism is *wird*, a homophone of "weird."

realm may such sciences be called "magical." Since the gateway of *tariqah* is not the only way of accessing the psychic realm, as we have seen, these magical sciences may indeed be adopted for ends quite inimical to spirituality.[2]

The writings of Shaykh Abd al-Wahid Yahya are generally concerned with principles rather than secondary expressions, and yet he did turn his attention to the cosmological or intermediary sciences. He describes in passing the science of Jafr as "an application of these same sciences to the prevision of future events; and this application...exhibits all the rigor of an exact and mathematical science for those who can understand and interpret it (for it possesses a kind of "cryptography," which in fact is no more astonishing than algebraic notation)."[3] Now, Herbert presents his work as an "effort at prediction," and in an unpublished interview he reveals his thoughts on prediction, and seems to guess at the science of Jafr:

> You see, I contend that there is such a thing...that you can do it, whether you do it by a subliminal thing...or whether it is...accumulating data. Or something mystical in a sense that it is unexplained thus far...I'm looking at it through Western eyes now as you'll undoubtedly see...that it is a mechanical scientific principle and if you get enough data to bear on it, you'll understand it...[4]

---

[2] For a recent example of the magical manipulation of politics, see Gary Lachman, *Dark Star Rising: Magick and Power in the Age of Trump*, New York: TarcherPerigee, 2018. Unfortunately, however, the author is ill-prepared to evaluate the truth of René Guénon.
[3] Guénon 2004.
[4] Herbert and McNally 1969.

In order to place Herbert's effort at prediction in its proper context, Guénon should be quoted at greater length:

> ...the word "prophecy" can only be properly used of the announcements of future events contained in the Sacred Books of the various traditions, and proceeding from an inspiration of a purely spiritual order; any other use of the word is entirely misleading, "prediction" being the proper word to use in all other cases. Predictions may come from very various sources; at least some have been a result of the application of certain secondary traditional sciences, and these are certainly the most valid, but only on condition that their meaning can really be understood...As for the rest, in so far as there is anything authentic in them, it emanates almost exclusively from sincere but very partially "enlightened seers" who have experienced certain confused perception related more or less accurately to a future that is usually not at all clearly determined, particularly as to the date and the order of succession of events, and who have unconsciously mixed those perceptions with their own ideas and consequently expressed them still more confusedly...[5]

Herbert's effort may perhaps rightly be understood to belong to "the rest," since its relationship to recent events in Iraq indicates something authentic indeed, even while the author's own ideas can be confusing enough. For example, Herbert presents in his novel the term "adab" as "the

---

[5] Guénon 1972.

demanding memory that comes upon you of itself." In reality, the Arabic word *adab* refers to "manners;" and in the language of Islamic esoterism, it refers more specifically to the spiritual exercises of an initiate. Moreover, a sacred reminder to maintain manners in the quest for the Divine - *adab ya Hu* - is traditionally posted in the Sufi lodges, enjoining proper respect for the Four Gateways.[6] In fact, the name "Muad'Dib" is from the same Arabic root and connotes a teacher, or in Herbert's words, "The One Who Points the Way;" but its meaning for Paul seems to relate more to "demanding memory," since it is bestowed upon him after he recalls his attention being drawn to the desert mouse of that name. No doubt the use of the term "prophet" further adds to confusion, given that *Dune's* terminology depends so profoundly upon Islamic conceptions that cannot allow for a prophet after Muhammad; but perhaps Herbert may be forgiven for this, since it would seem that he is simply following the example of the author of *The Sabres of Paradise*, who often enough and very mistakenly calls the Naqshbandi leader a prophet.

What is more important to consider is another term that Herbert introduces for his "off-world prophet," Lisan al-gaib. This title is translated as "The Voice from the Outer World," and indeed, its Arabic meaning is literally "tongue of the hidden," and so refers to what is outside the cosmic wall. Now, this title belonged historically to the Persian

---

[6] The Divine Name *Hu* may also appear on the exterior walls of Sufi lodges in southern Europe, and since its calligraphic form in Arabic is spiraling in design, this motif may very well relate to the ancient use of labyrinthine designs to protect houses in the same region against unwanted psychic influences (see Guénon, "Frameworks and Labyrinths," *Symbols of Sacred Science*, Hillsdale: Sophia Perennis, 2004). For examples of both this monumental calligraphy and the aforementioned sacred formula in a Naqshbandi context, see Algar, "Some Notes on the Naqshbandi Tariqat in Bosnia," *Studies in Comparative Religion*, volume 9 number 2, Spring 1975.

poet Hafez, and it is even claimed that he received this title from the Naqshbandi master Jami "on account of the spiritual knowledge displayed in his writing." [7] What demands our attention here is the rather remarkable fact that the verses of Hafez specifically serve in a practice of bibliomantic prediction, and this fact is so well established in Islamic culture that the use of his poetry in this practice has its own designation: *fal-i Hafez*. The name "Hafez" refers to a person who has preserved the Sacred Book of Islam to memory, and so *fal-i Hafez* may be considered among the secondary sciences, since it proceeds from a science of the Qur'an that must be considered to be of primary character. In any case, Herbert's use of this particular title betrays a very specific awareness of a science of prediction in Islam.

Muad'Dib's attainment of the rank of Lisan al-gaib fulfills the Bene Gesserit expectation of the Kwisatz Haderach, the "Shortening of the Way;" and this name is obviously adapted from the Kabbalistic term *kefitzat haderech* of the same meaning. It is curious that Herbert introduces here a Hebrew expression, but it may be offered that this term is used to approximate a station that the Bene Gesserit cannot reach or even properly identify. In other words, we are truly meant here to understand a spiritual realization beyond the psychic. This realization is accompanied by powers beyond the psychic abilities of the witches,[8] and so Herbert has "shortening of the way" signify "one who can be many places at once."

Remarkably, if we turn yet again to the Daghestani chain of the Naqshbandi way, we find six particular powers attained through spiritual realization, and one of these is

---

[7] *Hafez of Shiraz: Selections from his Poems*, translated by Herman Bicknell, London: Tubner, 1875, page xv.

[8] Herbert similarly includes the term "baraka" as the word for "a living holy man with magical powers," and the Arabic word refers to specifically spiritual influences.

known as the power of "folding" (*haqiqat ut-tayy*).[9] In describing this power of "folding space," a Naqshbandi authority makes the following claim: "High-level saints are able to be in 12,000 places in one time," and the example of Bayazid Bistami is cited; "Low-level saints can move and appear in two or three places at the same time."[10] Now, it is only in *Heretics of Dune* in 1984 that Herbert would use the expression "space-folding" in reference to the Guild Navigators; and in the very same year, the film *Dune* depicts the Guild Navigators monstrously transformed by the spice having the resultant power of "folding space." What is especially strange is that the expression "folding space" becomes more ingrained in Herbert's imaginary landscape over time, even though it becomes wrongly associated with a rank quite inferior to the Lisan al-gaib.[11]

This insistence of an idea, however, may be compared with the author's own Jungian concept of adab as a "demanding memory," only here the "demand" may rather be rooted in spiritual truth. Indeed, such a right belongs in some measure to all the spiritual realities that Herbert presents in his imaginary context, and especially the reality of the name "Mahdi" by which the Fremen identify the Lisan al-gaib; and as we hope to establish, this is not a "memory" reaching Herbert from the past.

---

[9] Another of these six powers, that of "outpouring" (*haqiqat ul-fayd*), is echoed in the name of Muad'Dib's nemesis, Feyd Rautha. The appearance of this term in this context would be inexplicable, if not for Muad'Dib's teaching that "He who can destroy a thing has the real control of it;" and so his ability to destroy Feyd might be interpreted as indicating his control of the "power of *fayd*."

[10] Shaykh Muhammad Hisham Kabbani, *The Sufi Science of Self-Realization*, Louisville: Fons Vitae, 2006, pages 220-35.

[11] This power should not be simply equated with the idea of a wormhole, even though "space-folds" are an integral part of it, since the wormhole is held to exist independently of the manipulation of space. In fact, the attention given to wormholes belongs rather to the matter of "holes in the cosmic wall."

5

Sun of Atreus

The destruction of the barrier against Gog and Magog is one of the five greater Indications of the End of Time according to Islamic prophecy. The other five include the appearance of the Antichrist, the appearance of the "Beast of the Earth," the descent of Jesus, and the "rising of the sun from the place of its setting." This last indication refers above all to the appearance of the expected leader named Muhammad al-Mahdi who marshals the faithful against the deceptions of the Antichrist. This identification of the Mahdi with the "western sun" is expressed, for example, in the title of the eschatological work of the Greatest Master Ibn `Arabi, the `Anqa' mughrib fi ma`rifat khatm al-awliya' wa shams al-maghrib ("The Wondrous `Anqa' in the Knowledge of the Seal of Sainthood and the Sun of the West").

It is not at first apparent how this association relates to Frank Herbert's formulation of the Mahdi of the Fremen, yet there is indeed a remarkable relationship that has gone unnoticed until now. To begin with, it should come as no surprise that Herbert admitted to having a Classical reference in mind with his choice of the name Atreides.[1] In Greek, "Atreides" signifies the "son of Atreus," and so most immediately refers to Agamemnon or Menelaus, although a more distant descendant could be indicated, as is the case here. The wise Plato mentions a "right of Atreus"

---

[1] In his *God Emperor of Dune*, Herbert has House Atreides trace its ancestry "directly back to the Greek original."

concerning the directions of the sunrise and sunset in *The Statesman*, and in mythology, Zeus reverses the course of the sun in the sky for Atreus. We are confronted here with a very curious coincidence. The reversing of the sun in its course belongs both to Classical mythology and Islamic prophecy, and the choice of Atreides as the name of the Mahdi in *Dune* suggests that Herbert was well aware of this. [2] If not, this connection should be considered a remarkably inspired coincidence.

There is also, of course, the well-known example of a similar miracle in the Bible belonging to Joshua, the successor of Moses.[3] The Book of Joshua relates that the sun and moon were stopped by Divine command in response to his prayer, so that his victory against the Amorites could be accomplished in the light of day. Now, concerning the Amorites, it should be recognized that the king of the Amorites in the time of Moses was the legendary giant Og, and some sources have even mistakenly replaced the name Og with Gog. However, Gog and Magog are themselves traditionally described "both as giants and as dwarfs;" that is, in unbalanced forms; and since "in all such symbolisms the same kind of "infra-corporeal" subtle influences are really always involved,"[4] the phonetic similarity between Og and Gog and Magog may be more than accidental. In

---

[2] Also, the name of Paul's father, Leto, is strangely the same as that of the *mother* of Apollo, but this only confirms the solar aspect.

[3] It may be worth noting that just as Joshua is under the authority of Moses, so is Atreus dependent upon Zeus, and the planet Jupiter – named for the Roman Zeus – is assigned specifically to the spirituality of Moses in Islamic esoterism.

[4] Guénon 1972, page 206-7. It should be noted that it is precisely the matter of "giants and dwarfs" that so preoccupies contemporary imaginations, and we have in mind especially the "interdimensional" aliens and the antediluvian giants. Of course, the giant Og is a traditional example of the latter, and is identified as such by his Arabic name `Uj bin `Anaq, that is, "Og, descendant of the Anakim."

the Qur'an, it is particularly Joshua's fearlessness in confronting giants that is mentioned.[5] Very curiously, the Qur'anic word for giant, *jabbar*, is employed by Herbert for the "gom jabbar," the "high handed enemy" of the Bene Gesserit that Paul Atreides must confront precisely to overcome his fear; and this occurs in the very first pages of the novel, and so sets its stage.

In the lands of Islam, the memory of the miracle of Joshua has remarkably been transferred to a Greek setting. Above the Bosporus near the city of Istanbul, there is a height known formerly as Jebar Dagh ("Giant's Mountain") and now as Yusha Dagh (the "Mountain of Joshua") on account of a tomb found there. The grave would seem to be that of an ancient giant, but travelers to its mosque observed a writing indicating its owner to be Joshua the son of Nun,[6] even though other resting places for this prophet exist: "'Now while his excellency Joshua, on a certain day, fought with this nation, in the first battle the sun went down on account of the Greeks, but while he was fighting the sun rose again after it had gone down, and the Greeks could not be saved.'"[7] Because of the presence of this sacred site inherited from Ottoman Constantinople, Joshua remains as one of the protecting saints of Istanbul. Since the Bosporus is the legendary location of the Symplegades, an

---

[5] V, 22-3. Joshua also figures in the Chapter of the Cave, that is, the same chapter that includes the account of the barrier against Gog and Magog. He is understood to be the unnamed youth in the story of the meeting of Moses with al-Khidr. The latter is described as having *"knowledge from Our presence"* (XVIII, 65), and if we recall the doctrine of the Four Gateways, this knowledge, evidently superior to that of Moses, may be understood to relate to the gateway of *haqiqah*. It may also be observed that al-Khidr instructs Moses in one instance by repairing a wall.

[6] The name Nūn is likewise that of the Arabic letter that corresponds to the sphere of the Sun in Islamic Hermeticism.

[7] Cf. F.W. Hasluck, *Christianity and Islam Under the Sultans, volume I*, Oxford: Clarendon Press, 1929, pages 304-8.

archetypal gateway between worlds, it may perhaps be understood that the spiritual presence of Joshua ensures the integrity of this gateway, with the psychic danger embodied in the ancient giant having been overcome by spirituality.[8]

The role of Joshua has been described as being that of "proto-eschatological conqueror,"[9] a description that could easily be applied to the conquering Atreides of Herbert's imagination. Of course, there is no conqueror so renowned as Alexander, the "Lord of the Twin Horns;" whose title "is most often interpreted in the sense of a double power extending over both the East and the West."[10] East and west define a solar dimension, and it is significant that the Qur'an relates his travels to the "setting place of the sun" and the "rising place of the sun" before his arrival at the twin peaks to build his wall.[11] The "Western Sun" of Islam likewise promises conquest, especially of Rome, and the Greatest Shaykh Ibn `Arabi hints at the link between the

---

[8] This situation may even be compared to the mythology of the founding of Britain. When the Trojans under Brutus arrived in ancient Albion, they found it inhabited by giants, but the victory of Corineus over the last giant "Goemagog" made the land safe; and so Britain is named after the Trojan commander, and Cornwall, the western limit of Britain and home of Goemagog, is named for Corineus. Now, what is especially remarkable is that effigies of Corineus and Goemagog are to this day assigned a protective role for London, the city held to have been founded by Brutus. Unfortunately, their names have suffered such confusion that these guardians of London are now called Gog and Magog. For his part, William Blake was rather preoccupied with the giants of ancient Albion.

[9] Gerald T. Elmore, *Islamic Sainthood in the Fullness of Time: Ibn al-`Arabi's Book of the Fabulous Gryphon*, Leiden: Brill, 1999, page 177.

[10] René Guénon, "The Symbolism of Horns," in *Symbols of Sacred Science*, op. cit.

[11] XVIII, 85-91. For that matter, Mashu of Mesopotamian mythology is a mountain of two peaks associated with the resting place of the sun.

Mahdi and Dhul-Qarnayn with his book of the `Anqa' mughrib, since it is actually a "sequel" to his *Tadbirat al-ilahiyya fi islah al-mamlakat al-insaniyya* ("Divine Governance of the Human Kingdom") that in turn was modeled upon the guidance Aristotle gave to Alexander the Great. Still, it must be insisted that the Mahdi or "Rightly-guided" is more than an eschatological conqueror.

In the most authentic Traditions (*ahadith*), the Mahdi is the expected one who *"fills the earth with equality and justice, as it has been filled with injustice and oppression."* He is the most pure descendant of the Messenger Muhammad, who is also reported to have said, *"At the end of my Nation al-Mahdi will come for whom Allah sends rain and the earth produces its plants..."* This contrasts with the anticipated intrusion of Gog and Magog into this world, when they are expected to consume and destroy all resources, especially water; and this is perhaps the most relevant Tradition to Herbert's ecological vision, since Muad'Dib is expected to transform the desert.

Al-Mahdi is called the Caliph or "Representative" of God, so he represents Divine Truth in the time of the Antichrist or Deceiver (*Dajjal*) who is the counterfeit of Jesus; and even though Jesus, who is the Spirit of God (*Ruhullah*), descends to slay his imposter, it should be clear that until that descent, the ability to discriminate between the spiritually authentic and illusions that deceive the soul is important indeed. Among all names, "Mahdi" indicates spiritual safety in the time leading to the apocalypse; it is the name indicated in the prophecies of the Messenger Muhammad, and these prophecies should not be played with.[12] The realities of the words and names that Herbert invokes simply do not belong to him.

---

[12] The banner of the Mahdi is known to be black, and so counterfeit black banners have already appeared, most recently with ISIS. Herbert consistently describes the banners of Muad'Dib as black and green; but since it is understood that the banner of the

Sun of Atreus

Just as the spiritual world transcends the `alam ul-mithal*, the reality of al-Mahdi may be properly understood neither through Jungian speculations nor the taking of hallucinogenic drugs. Obviously, President Kennedy was in no wise King Arthur, and so Herbert may have been right to warn people against confusing a man with a myth; but if Paul-Muad'Dib actually attains the Water of Life and becomes rightly identified with the Lisan al-gaib and Mahdi – which he does on all counts – he should be free of the confusion that Herbert insists upon; and if Muad'Dib is truly a son of Atreus, he must therefore also be the "Sun of the West" for the Fremen and not an imposter.

No doubt Frank Herbert discovered a trace of spiritual authenticity through the account of the Murid Wars that inspired him. Yet the specific spirituality of the Murids must be seen to have much more than an incidental relevance in these matters, since it is claimed in Naqshbandi sources that "*Al-Mahdi will be one of the followers of this way.*"[13] So even the idea of bringing Naqshbandi traditions into an eschatological scenario was not Herbert's. It might, however, be glimpsed in the histories of the *Rashahat `ayn al-hayat*, such as when the sun waited in the sky for Khwaja Ahrar who was even instructed by the spirituality of Jesus.

In modern times, the Daghestani master of Shaykh Nazim al-Haqqani promised: *"He who makes a regular*

Mahdi is inherited from the Messenger Muhammad, it is perhaps worth considering that the caliphs of the Prophet have historically preserved his sacred black banner with green reinforcements. As far as the followers of ISIS are concerned, they have cut themselves off from the spiritual world through their rejection of Sufism, and allowed themselves to be deceived.

[13] Shaykh Muhammad Hisham Kabbani, *The Naqshbandi Sufi Way: The History and Guidebook of the Saints of the Golden Chain*, Chicago: Kazi, 1995, page 237. Concerning the "caliphal inheritance" of the only order that includes Abu Bakr As-Siddiq, see *Alchemy in Middle-earth*, page 89; this very distinction is parodied by the name of ISIS' false caliph, Abu Bakr al-Baghdadi.

practice of the Adab and the Awrad shall obtain the water of true life and...he will bathe in it and drink it, and by means of it shall he reach his goal." Clearly this promise resonates with the story of Muad'Dib (from the same root as *adab*) and the weirding way (*awrad* is the plural of *wird*); but what makes the specific spiritual elements of *Dune* even more significant, and what may not be found in the account of the Murid Wars, is the further assurance that this Naqshbandi teaching specifically *"pertains to the time leading up to the appearance of our Master Muhammad al-Mahdi (on whom be peace!)."*[14] In this light, *Dune* appears to pertain to this time for reasons beyond the vision of its author.

Sultan ul-awliya[15] Shaykh `Abdullah Daghestani
Master of the Naqshbandi Golden Chain when *Dune* appeared

---

[14] Op. cit., pages 36 and 13.
[15] Rather inexplicably, Herbert glosses "auliya" – the plural form of the Arabic word for "saints" (literally, "friends") - as "the female at the left hand of God; God's handmaiden." Needless to say, if Herbert has proven himself unfamiliar with the *`alam ul-arwah*, he must obviously be ignorant of the realm beyond the gateway of *haqiqah*.

6

Buddislam?

Frank Herbert's invention of the term "Buddislam," while problematic to say the least, invites inquiry into what is truly indicated by the meeting of Buddhism and Islam. Obviously, there is not room here to examine the history of this encounter, except to note that it was not characterized by the sort of conflicts that Islam would face against Christianity and Hinduism, and that Islam in Central Asia far more effortlessly succeeded to Buddhism there. The establishment of the Naqshbandi and Qadiri Sufi orders over the Chinese borderlands has been traced to Afaq Khoja, who was an ally of the Fifth Dalai Lama and whose disciples included many former followers of Lamaism.[1]

Above all, however, it must be insisted that there can be no question of any sort of fusion of religious forms such as Herbert imagines, even in the context of long passages of time. Indeed, such speculations deny the very nature of things. Religious forms are but more or less direct emanations of the permanent Primordial Tradition, and so they may be understood to be united at their source; but just as all temporal things may be said to move towards decay, even a single religious tradition moves away from integrity and not towards it. Adding one religious form to another does not bring metaphysical unity any closer.[2]

---

[1] On the subject of the Naqshbandi order in China, see especially the excellent works of Joseph Fletcher.
[2] Even so, there is a physical convergence of Buddhism and Islam in the example of the footprint in stone atop Adam's Peak in Sri

What is more, Buddhism even began as a "rupture" separating from a more ancient tradition, in this case Hinduism, although much the same observation may be made for the separate example of Christianity. Still, Hinduism allows for the legitimacy of Buddhism through the doctrine of the avatars of Vishnu, with the historical Buddha being identified as the ninth or "foreign" (*mleccha*) avatar.[3] The designation "foreign" may therefore be understood as referring not to the avatar's origin, but rather to the domain of influence; and indeed, the historical expression of Buddhism occurs predominantly outside India. Yet this expansion into foreign lands established Buddhism in an intermediary position between the Hindu tradition and the tradition of ancient China, the latter comprising both Confucianism that addresses secular affairs and Taoism that is concerned with the psychic and spiritual domains. So Chinese or Chan Buddhism arose; and when reaching Japan, this Chinese form was called Zen, the form most familiar to Frank Herbert. For him, "Zensunni" was the main form of "Buddislam."

There is another way in which Buddhism may be understood to have an intermediary role. In the article "Hermes," René Guénon notes how the name "Buddha" is related to the Sanskrit name for Mercury, and that the Buddha was appropriately illuminated by this planet.[4]

Lanka, and the two traditions more generally share an emphasis on the symbolism of the sacred footprint. For examples from the American Indian world in the context of Muslim veneration, see *The Red and the White*, chapter 6.

[3] The meaning of "avatar" relates to "descent;" for this reason, the Messenger of Islam may not be identified as "merely" an avatar, since his appearance included not only spiritual descent, but also ascent, as demonstrated in the "Night Journey and Ascension" (*laylat ul-isra' wal-mi`raj*).

[4] This article has been included in *Traditional Forms and Cosmic Cycles* (Hillsdale: Sophia Perennis, 2003), and includes still more reasons to associate the Buddha with Mercury.

Buddislam?

While Mercury is obviously identical to Hermes, the Divine messenger, this association between Buddhism and Classical mythology is actually far from arbitrary. The early development of Buddhist iconography is associated above all with the Gandhara region and the artistic school known as "Greco-Buddhist" that was made possible through the conquests of Alexander the Great. Be that as it may, none other than Hermes is depicted alongside representations of the Buddha in Greco-Buddhist art.[5] It is worth observing that Hermes appears especially in the scene known as the "Donation of the Four Bowls by the Guardians of the World," that is, the story concerning the origin of the sacred bowl of the Buddha.

The importance of this relic in Buddhism has invited comparisons with the Holy Grail,[6] yet what has been overlooked is the particularly Hermetic aspect of their correspondence, even though the Hermetic Krater has independently been offered as a prototype for the Grail. What concerns us here is that the legend of the Grail was attributed in the Middle Ages to an Arabic account of a certain Flegetanis, and there can be no doubt that what is indicated by the name "Flegetanis" is actually *falak uth-thani*, the heavenly sphere of Mercury in Arabic terminology.[7] According to the perspective shared by the

---

[5] Hercules also appears in this artistic milieu, and the incorporation of Hercules into Buddhist iconography extends even to Japan and the example of its Nio guardians. The Bamyan statues destroyed by the Wahhabi Taliban in 2001 – along with countless others - belonged to this Gandharan artistic tradition. It should also be mentioned that the five Buddhist monks of the title, *Fusang: The Discovery of America by Chinese Buddhist Monks in the Fifth Century*, were from Gandhara.

[6] Cf. Alfred Nutt, "The Legend of the Buddha's Alms Dish and the Legend of the Holy Grail." *Archaeological Review*, 3, 4 June 1889

[7] Cf. Kahane, *The Krater and the Grail: Hermetic Sources of the Parzival*, Urbana: University of Illinois Press, 1965. For the proper significance of the name Flegetanis, however, as well as of the

Christian and Islamic traditions, the intermediary or secondary sciences are also known as the Hermetic sciences, since they are traced to Hermes and therefore related to this same planetary sphere.

We have already mentioned that for the world of the human microcosm, the soul serves in an intermediary capacity between the spirit and body. As far as Buddhism is concerned, given its intermediary role, it should come as no surprise that it is characterized by meditative practices, or rather methods designed to discipline the soul, including celibacy. This observation may, in fact, account for an aspect of Buddhism that confounds modern observers, namely its "non-theism." Rather than being a source of confusion, this aspect of Buddhism may simply serve to remind us that the world of the soul is not to be confused with the spiritual world. In this connection, it is worth observing that Islamic esoterism assigns the sphere of Mercury to Jesus, who as mentioned before is nothing less than the Spirit of God, and perhaps this assignation compensates for the psychic emphasis of the intermediary sciences.[8]

Concerning the matter of religious practices in *Dune*, the powers of the Bene Gesserit are based on what is called "prana-bindu." This term is actually a combination of Sanskrit words, the first of which signifies "breath" that is also the literal meaning of the Arabic word for "soul" (*nafs*). The second word, *bindu*, seems even less significant, since it literally means "point," but both terms in fact have a special relevance in Tantric Buddhism. *Bindu* particularly identifies the *chakra* located at the base of the skull where the substance called *amrita* is collected. Now, *amrita* derives

---

Grail itself, we must turn to Pierre Ponsoye's *L'Islam et le Graal* (Milan: Arche, 1976).

[8] Similarly, the personality of Hermes is assimilated in Islam to the antediluvian prophet Idris, who is assigned the chief position in the spiritual hierarchy of Islamic esoterism. Cf. *The Red and the White*, chapter 5.

Buddislam?

from the same root as the word "ambrosia," and this word may even be related to the Grail symbolism indicated above, since the presence of the Grail in England is traditionally attributed to Saint Joseph of Arimathea whose place of origin is composed of the same letters. What is indeed relevant here is that when the Hindu Tantric text *Amritakunda* ("Pool of Nectar") was translated into Arabic by Medieval Sufis, it was rendered as *Hawd ul-hayat* ("Pool of the Water of Life"). According to this text, three are especially associated with the Water of Life: al-Khidr, Elijah,[9] and the "Lord of the Fish" Jonah, whose title recalls the Fisher King of Grail lore. In any case, the very presence of this text in Sufi circles[10] – and it was indeed widespread – proves that in addition to the recognized incorporation of Tantra into Hinduism and Buddhism, there is such a thing as "Islamic Tantrism" in much the same way that we may speak of Christian and Islamic Hermeticism.

One reason for the ignorance concerning this subject in the Islamic milieu is that its existence is not labelled with the Sanskrit word *tantra*; at the same time, it is true that the terms associated with its methods are themselves controversial and ill-understood. One of these pertinent terms in Islamic esoterism is *qalandar*, and while the origin of this word is obscure,[11] its purported meaning

---

[9] On the association of al-Khidr and Elijah as chiefs of the spiritual hierarchy, see *The Red and the White* chapter 5; they are said to defend the barrier against Gog and Magog every night "until the Mahdi appears" (Van Donzel and Schmidt, page 110). For the association of Elijah with al-Mahdi, see *Alchemy in Middle-earth*, page 84.

[10] Although this Tantric influence did not originate with the Shattari Sufi order, it became inseparable from it, and so it is of interest to observe that the Arabic word *shattar* signifies the "swift," that is, a principal attribute of Hermes/Mercury.

[11] The origin of *qalandar* likely belongs to the "Syrian" language, which in Islamic esoterism indicates the primordial solar language.

refers to "pure gold," and this may no doubt be compared with the Hermetic language of alchemy.[12] The other term we have in mind is *malamah* and its associated forms, from an Arabic root relating to "blame." The usage of these terms is essentially interchangeable, while each term actually has a dual and contrasting significance in itself. On the one hand, these words may indicate blameworthy antinomian behavior, and therefore conduct unfit for *tariqah* since even *shari`ah* is being disrespected. On the other hand, these words refer to a rank above that of the Sufis, with the people of *malamah* specifically being identified as the people of *ma`rifah*.[13] This situation may indeed be compared with the confusions attached to the word *tantra*, since it too may indicate unlawful behavior, or a teaching of primary importance recognized as the "fifth Veda."

In all these cases, however, it is important to observe that such confusions have arisen from misappropriation. Masters of *tariqah* insisted that those "who took the dress of *qalandaris* in order to indulge in debaucheries are not to be confused with true *qalandaris*."[14] Respect for the Four Gateways ensured the truth of the "Tantric" methods in Islam, and prevented these methods from serving rather to subvert spiritual realization. The need for these methods to be attached to the highest spiritual authority is precisely why the Tantric text *Hawd ul-hayat* has been attributed to the Greatest Master of Islamic

---

[12] On the relationship between Hindu Tantrism and alchemy, see Titus Burckhardt, *Alchemy: Science of the Cosmos, Science of the Soul*, Shaftesbury: Element, 1986.

[13] This identification appears in "Principes des Malâmatiyah," translated by Ivan Aguéli in *Écrits pour La Gnose*, (Milano: Arché, 1988, page 73). Cf. more generally the appendix "Sufis, Malamatis, and Qalandaris" in Trimingham's *The Sufi Orders in Islam* (Oxford: Oxford University Press, 1971). Ultimately there would be established separate Sufi orders specifically named "Qalandari" and "Malami."

[14] Ibid., page 268.

esoterism, Ibn ʿArabi, an attribution that is otherwise inexplicable. Again, as far as *Dune* is concerned, the Tantrism of the Bene Gesserit is not tied to the spiritual world, and so the tau sex orgy appears as a decidedly antinomian expression.

According to the true meaning of *malamah*, "blame" is attached to everything relating to the domain of the *nafs*.[15] We have already encountered this attitude in the teachings of the Daghestani lineage of the Naqshbandi way, concerning the "remorse" of the seeker for "having pursued stations and states" of the psychic realm in *tariqah* rather than the spiritual goal. Indeed, the Naqshbandi master Muhammad Parsa observed that "whatever holds true of the Malamatis holds true of our masters (*khwajagan*) also."[16] We have also had occasion to mention Bayazid al-Bistami concerning the power of "folding space," and to this same master "is ascribed the formulation of the specific doctrines of this school."[17] One of the distinctive methods of this "school" concerns five spiritual faculties (*lata'if*) that transcend the *nafs* and that are nonetheless associated with specific points in the human anatomy. Obviously, this concept may be compared with the Tantric *chakras*, including the aforementioned *bindu*, and therefore also the "elixir fields" of Taoist alchemy (*neidan*); yet there is not an exact correlation between these systems. Even when the location on the body happens to coincide, there is still the question of whether this point serves as a support for the presence of the *ruh* or only the *nafs*.[18] In any case, it is worth

---

[15] No doubt this attitude may be compared with that of Diogenes the Cynic who counseled Alexander the Great.

[16] Quoted in "Malamatiyya," *Encyclopaedia of Islam*, Leiden: Brill, 1991.

[17] Trimingham, page 265.

[18] Cf. Arthur F. Buehler, *Sufi Heirs of the Prophet*, Columbia: University of South Carolina Press, 1998, page 110. Correspondingly, there are points on the "body" of the earth that may serve as supports for psychic, and more rarely spiritual,

observing that the *qalandars* who introduced Sufism into Europe were often affiliated with these same masters (*khwajagan*), and that despite the Islamic orthodoxy of these masters, the customs of the *qalandars* are very often indistinguishable from those of the Tantric Buddhists.[19]

The historic and intermediary role of what might be termed a "Buddh" dimension of Islam may be glimpsed through the following example. The *qalandar* Khidr Rumi is held to have possessed a miraculous cup, recalling the relics associated above with the sphere of Mercury; his disciple Najmuddin is purported to have journeyed twice to England and China, and whose life of two centuries suggests something of the Water of Life.[20] This particular link between the Far East and West in the High Middle Ages may provide an explanation for a remarkable comparison noted in passing by René Guénon in *The Reign of Quantity*. On the opposite page, the image above is from western China subsequent to the introduction of Buddhism, and the image below appears in the context of Hermeticism in Europe. Of course, the role of Islam in transmitting Hermetic teachings into Europe is incontestable. In this instance, that the first image served as inspiration for the second through an Islamic transmission may hardly be doubted.

---

influences, and this relates to what was noted earlier concerning "portals."

[19] See above all the formidable work of Emil Esin, for example the article "Thèmes et symbols communs entre le Bouddhisme Tantrique et la tradition des Bektachis Ottomans." Thierry Zarcone identifies a "Qalandari-Naqshbandi" spiritual current in his article, "Histoire et croyances des derviches turkestanais et indiens à Istanbul" (*Anatolia Moderna*, Paris, 1990), in which he also proposes that the distinctive custom of the so-called "celibate" branch of the Bektashi order arises not from Christian inspiration but rather Buddhist (page 185).

[20] John A. Subhan, *Sufism: Its Saints and Shrines*, Lucknow: Lucknow Publishing, 1938, pages 311-2.

Buddislam?

**Above: Fuxi and Nüwa
Below: "Rebis" attributed to Basil Valentine**

The knowledge being transmitted concerns a balance of complementary forces, and the serpent or dragon identifies its psychic context; the central position of Mercury among the planets is clear in the latter example. Complementary terms are indicated by the compasses and square that are emblems of the sky and the earth, as well as by the masculine and feminine forms [21] that are the primordial twins Fuxi and Nüwa in the Chinese example.[22]

These very brief indications deserve a much fuller treatment, and other examples could in fact be found, but we should finally return to Paul-Muad'Dib's realization in *Dune*. His vision through the "Water of Life" surpasses that of the Bene Gesserit because he gains knowledge of both the "force that gives" and the "force that takes" that are specifically associated with the feminine and masculine. In the Cave of Birds, when Muad'Dib is asked if he is "one who gives or one who takes," he replies: "I'm at the fulcrum," and so refers to that which must be present to bring contrasting pairs into balance and ensure stability in the psychic domain.

---

[21] The noticeable juxtaposition of square and compasses has been addressed by René Guénon in *The Great Triad* (Cambridge: Quinta Essentia, 1991, chapter 15). Concerning the masculine and feminine, it may be observed that while sexual gender is an obviously physical expression, the attainment of balance in the psychic realm should not be confused with a hermaphroditic condition; after all, in the original example, the separate twins are physically male and female. Mocking psychic balance, the Antichrist appears traditionally as a hermaphrodite.

[22] In Chinese mythology, Nüwa is held to have repaired a tear in the sky using stones of five colors. Guénon considers this to be an ancient example of a fissure in the "Great Wall" (Guénon 1972, page 207). It is of interest to note that each of the five spiritual faculties *(lata'if)* mentioned above is associated with a different color.

7

Shai-hulud

Like the Rebis, the Roman Janus is depicted with two faces, and Frank Herbert admitted to incorporating Janus symbolism in his story.[1] This symbolism pertains especially to doorways, with the Latin word for doorway (*janua*) deriving from the name Janus. According to its temporal symbolism, the two faces of Janus look respectively to the past and to the future; yet there is in fact an invisible "third" face that pertains to the present. The invisibility of this face expresses the transcendence of the present that reconciles the other opposing perspectives.[2] Herbert includes this superior perspective as "the spread out *present*, its limits extended into the future and into the past" in his description of the attainment of Paul-Muad'Dib in the Cave of Birds.

The keystone of an arch may represent such a superior and unifying presence that stabilizes the opposing sides of a door. In a remarkable example from Iraq, the Gate of the Talisman in Baghdad formerly depicted two dragons in its archway, with a haloed (and therefore luminous) hero between them.[3]

---

[1] Brian Herbert, op. cit., page 178.

[2] Cf. Guénon, "Some Aspects of the Symbolism of Janus," *Symbols of Sacred Science*, op. cit.

[3] It is worth considering that this image was demolished in 1917 at the end of Ottoman rule, and since the Ottoman caliphs were representatives of the Prophet, this coincidence is not without significance. The loss of spiritual authority over political affairs in Iraq would have to bring with it psychic and physical imbalance,

Mysteries of *Dune*

The Talisman Gate in Iraq

The coiled tails of the dragons may be compared with the serpentine bodies of the Chinese primordial twins. The dragons are not allowed to separate from the hero but are held in perfect balance; and in the Chinese example, the serpent is even more explicitly bound to the human form. The significance of this relationship is contained in the curious Arabic saying with which Shaykh Abd al-Wahid Yahya opens his article on "Seth:" "*Kāna l-insānu hayyatan fil-qidām*," meaning, "Man was originally a serpent."[4] The term *qidām* does not simply indicate the past as opposed to the future, but contains rather the idea of "primordiality."[5] The saying emphasizes that the primordial and therefore

---

at least eventually; and so the entrance of ISIS onto the world stage as a twisted mockery of this authority was only a matter of time.
[4] *Symbols of Sacred Science*, op. cit.
[5] In Islamic esoterism, the Primordial Human is termed *al-insān al-qadīm*.

spiritual state is characterized by integration in the psychic domain. No doubt the restoration of this state is made possible, in Tantric terms, by the power known as *kundalini*, a term that signifies the coiled form of a serpent.

Any symbol has a luminous or tenebrous aspect. The sinister connotations of the imagery on page 27 may therefore be seen as but the mockery of the luminous aspect of "riding the dragon,"[6] and so Muad'Dib's riding of the sandworm may rather be an expression of this aspect. In general, the serpent or dragon may alternatively be associated with the integration of the primordial state or with a rebellion against it. This may be compared with the tall stature and longevity attributed by the Abrahamic traditions to the paradisal condition, but that also characterizes the rebellious antediluvian giants. We have seen that a tyrannical giant was replaced by the victorious spirituality of Joshua in the Bosporus, but that the dimensions of Joshua's tomb indicates that its owner is likewise a giant.

A comparable process is discernible in the tales told throughout the Balkans of the *qalandari* shaykh Sari Saltiq slaying a seven-headed dragon. Following his victory, the saint takes up residence in the dragon's cave and is ultimately interred in seven different coffins, embodying his symbolic relationship with the dragon.[7] Of course, the archetype of the dragon slayer is Saint George, and so it is of tremendous significance that he is known in Islam as al-Khidr, the Green Man, the very saint who accompanied Alexander the Great and attained the Water of Life.[8]

---

[6] This motif appears especially in Taoism.

[7] Cf. Hasluck, chapter XXXII and passim. Hasluck suspected a correspondence between the accounts of the giant slayer Joshua and the dragon slayer Sari Saltiq, but could not comprehend its significance (page 308).

[8] Al-Khidr actually assists Sari Saltiq in his victory over the dragon.

These considerations enable us to turn our attention to the name Frank Herbert gives to the all-important dragons of Dune. The author glosses "Shai-hulud" as:

> Sandworm of Arrakis, the "Old Man of the Desert," "Old Father Eternity," and "Grandfather of the Desert." Significantly, this name...designates the earth deity of Fremen hearth superstitions. Sandworms grow to enormous size...and live to great age...

Although the name seems to be Arabic like so much of Herbert's terminology, there is no straightforward equivalent to be found, and so the borrowing appears indirect at best. Still, there is a consensus that the word "hulud" is simply the Arabic *khulūd*,[9] especially since this word contains the idea of "eternity" that Herbert includes in his definition. In seeking a direct translation of the word "shai," however, attempts have settled on the word for "thing," despite the lack of evidence that Herbert had this generic notion in mind. On the contrary, Herbert does give no less than three indications in his short definition that emphasize the idea of an elder man, that is, *shaykh* in Arabic or shaikh. Clearly the words begin with the same letters; the hyphen would then simply indicate an ellipsis of sorts in place of the last letter *kha* that is also the first letter of *khulūd*.[10]

---

[9] The substitution of h for the letter *kha* is not unknown in the adoption of Arabic words, for example by Turkic languages.

[10] At the same time, the ellipsis would also replace the last letters of "Shaitan," a name for the immortal Adversary that Herbert employs, as we have already seen. This ellipsis may then provide a deliberate ambiguity, with "Shai-hulud" signaling either primordiality or rebellion in keeping with the symbolism of the dragon.

Shai-hulud

We are left, then, with the name *shai(kh)-hulud*, or an "immortal shaykh," with "shaykh," as we have seen, designating a spiritual master in Sufism. Of course, only a master associated with the Water of Life could be considered to be an "ever-living master," and such is indeed among the names of al-Khidr in the Muslim world. It is therefore of great interest to recall that the name for "serpent" in the Arabic saying quoted above – *hayyah* – is in essence a word for "living;" while in *Dune*, the Water of Life is derived from "that liquid exhalation of the sandworm produced at the moment of its death." In other words, the finding of the Water of Life is synonymous with victory over the dragon or serpent, and both are attributes of the immortal shaykh al-Khidr who is also Saint George.[11]

The mysterious relationship between spiritual realization and Shai-hulud is mocked, however, through the principal plot development in Herbert's sequels. This development even has a name, the "Golden Path," that itself recalls the *tariqah* (literally "path") of the Naqshbandi Golden Chain that includes al-Khidr. On this Golden Path, the son of Paul-Muad'Dib merges with the sandworms; but instead of relating in some way to the recovery of the primordial condition, Leto II becomes tyrannical and monstrous as the "God Emperor" of Dune, with enormous size and great longevity. To be fair, such a dark formulation of the "dragon king" also belongs to the mythology of the lands of Islam, as is clear from the example of Zahhak in the Persian *Shah Nama* or "Book of Kings." With man-eating serpents rising from both shoulders, Zahhak's monstrous form contrasts with that of the hero of the Gate of the Talisman, since the serpents are not under control but rather in control of Zahhak. Nevertheless, it is important to

---

[11] Very remarkably, Herbert may be confirming that he has al-Khidr in mind with his reference to the "earth deity of Fremen hearth superstitions," since this phrase so clearly recalls the Neopagan veneration of the Green Man.

recognize that the overthrow of Leto II results in disintegration (the "Scattering"), whereas the overthrow of Zahhak brings the restoration of just rule in Faridun, a king of utmost integrity; and it is fascinating to recognize that Faridun is even able subsequently to assume the form of a dragon.[12]

Despite the partiality of Herbert's point of view, there is no denying the fact that the entry immediately before "SHAI-HULUD" in *Dune*'s Glossary of the Imperium is actually "SHAH-NAMA." The Persian epic holds much more concerning *Dune* than the account of Zahhak's overthrow, as it is among the earliest Islamic sources of the quest of Alexander the Great. As a consequence, Herbert would have found in the *Shah Nama* an account of the search for the Water of Life.[13] There can be little doubt, then, that the derivation of Shai-hulud suggested here belongs to the world of possibility, since the immortal shaykh al-Khidr holds the secret of the Water, just as the sandworm holds the secret of the spice.[14]

---

[12] Unlike the East, the Western world suffers a chronic inability to recognize the luminous aspect of dragon symbolism; nevertheless, King Arthur remains in the West the model of kingly chivalry, and he belongs to the lineage of Pen*dragon*.

[13] Of course, Herbert would also have found traces of al-Khidr in the writings of Henri Corbin.

[14] Still, the significance of the "missing" letter *kha* in Shai-hulud should not be ignored. It is, appropriately enough, the first letter of the Arabic name of the Green Man; and this letter may also stand for the Divine Name *al-Khabīr*, the Aware, in Islamic esoterism. Indeed, only through awareness of the spiritual master may the primordial state be won from the dragon.

8

Usul

Although his project was ultimately unrealized, the filmmaker Alejandro Jodorowsky tried to adapt *Dune* to the screen in the 1970s, and his dubious ambitions were amplified by what he recognized in the project's potential:

> I wanted to do a movie that would give the people who took LSD at that time the hallucinations that you get with that drug, but without hallucinating. I did not want LSD to be taken, I wanted to fabricate the drug's effects...So, what I wanted was to create a prophet, to change the young minds of all the world![1]

During the same period, some of the novel's elements would be successfully mined by George Lucas for his *Star Wars*, although the indebtedness to *Dune* is more apparent in the early drafts of his screenplay. "Aura spice" and the "Jedi-Bendu" were obviously inspired by concepts in Herbert's novel that we have already discussed, although

---

[1] Quotation taken from the trailer to the documentary *Jodorowsky's Dune*. It is worth noting that before turning to his *Dune* project, Jodorowsky was introduced to LSD by Oscar Ichazo, a teacher of Ennegram speculations. Remarkably, the Ennegram has been associated with the Naqshbandi order specifically, while its principal innovator, G.I. Gurdjieff, was of Transcaucasian origin, and has even been associated with a "path of blame."

these particular expressions came to be modified. The importance of a desert planet, of course, was preserved.[2]

As for the Jedi-Bendu, the name was simplified to Jedi, yet still their "arts" should be compared to pranabindu. There is, however, a more profound comparison to be made between the Jedi of *Star Wars* and motifs in *Dune*. As we have established in "The Balance of George Lucas' *Star Wars*," "Jedi" is above all else a reference to the ancient Egyptian Djed pillar, symbol of Osiris, with the rival "Sith" order indicating Osiris' brother Seth and the ruin he brings.[3] In *Dune*, one of Paul Atreides' principal names is Usul, that Herbert glosses as "base of the pillar." In actuality, this is not quite its meaning in Arabic, since *usul* relates rather specifically to the stability of a tree with its roots. The term commonly belongs to the domain of *shari`ah*, and is employed to refer to the fundamentals of religion rather than its branches. The symbolism of the tree extends beyond the *shari`ah*, however: the Qur'anic mention of *"a Blessed Tree…Neither of the East nor of the West"*[4] pertains especially to spirituality, and Shaykh Muhyiddin Ibn `Arabi praised the Prophet Muhammad as *Shajarat ul-kawn*, the "Cosmic Tree." While Herbert may have abandoned the arboreal aspect of *usul*, it should be allowed that he nonetheless preserves its axial significance.

---

[2] Like Jung and Corbin, Lucas' mentor Joseph Campbell was a participant in the Eranos Conference.

[3] Osiris is also the husband of Isis. In *Star Wars*, the twins Luke and Leia embody the cosmic forces that are most well-known as the yin and yang of the Chinese tradition that literally refer to the shady and sunny sides of a hill. While Luke etymologically refers to light, Leia approximates the name Leila, meaning "night" (certainly a better explanation than the claim that Lucas pays homage here to the Princess Alia of *Dune*); or again, just as the sky and earth are complementary, so too are the last names of the twins, Skywalker and Organa, since the latter recalls what is organic or earthly.

[4] XXIV, 35.

Usul

We have mentioned the need for a superior presence in order to bring complementary forces into balance, and this presence resides at the axis. Dune under the balanced rule of Usul promises to bring water to the desert, in fulfillment of the coming of House Atreides to Arrakis from watery Caladan. Sometimes these forces appear as opposites, as with the rival houses of Atreides and Harkonnen; yet still such oppositions are reconciled by the axis, and so Usul stands between these houses, since he is descended from both. Herbert eventually introduces male and female twins as the children of Paul-Muad'Dib.[5]

The above Chinese ideogram for "tree" (*mu*)[6] includes both branches above and roots below, centered and balanced on the vertical axis of the trunk. The tree's verticality may be compared to the axial significance of the *alif* in the Science of Letters (*`ilm ul-huruf*) of Islamic

---

[5] Lucas, of course, posits Luke and Leia as the twins of Anakin Skywalker; however, there is a confusing aspect to all this, since Anakin is not really balanced, although his twins may be understood to "bring balance," whereas Paul's twins are rather unbalanced, since Herbert chooses to undermine the legacy of Usul in his sequels, as we have seen in the example of Leto II.

[6] It is of great interest to note that this same Chinese ideogram appears in the petroglyphs of ancient America, especially in the West, since the ancient Chinese name for America was Fusang, in reference to the mythological Tree of the Sun. Cf. *The Red and the White*, chapter 7.

esoterism. [7] Also, the tree's structure of trunk and complementary branches finds microcosmic expression in Tantrism, in the doctrine of the three principal *nadis* of the human subtle form; their points of meeting are the *chakras*, and so include the *bindu*. Moreover, the same Chinese ideogram shares the form of the *vajra* or *dorje*, the thunderbolt weapon of Tantric Buddhism. Just as the names Usul and Jedi correspond, so may the latter's distinctive weapon, the lightsaber, be compared to the lightning aspect of the *vajra*. [8] Given the role of Usul as a "proto-eschatological conqueror," this symbolism suggests that the axial authority has the right to restore balance by force.

When George Lucas was looking for someone to direct the conclusion of his saga, *Return of the Jedi*, he offered the job to the acclaimed filmmaker David Lynch, who reportedly suggested that Lucas direct it himself. In any case, declining Lucas' offer, Lynch turned instead to the challenge of adapting *Dune*. The 1984 film was indeed completed with Lynch as both screenwriter and director, but only through artistic compromise and without his approval of its editing. [9] Most significantly, however,

---

[7] Comments offered earlier regarding Tantrism help explain how the Science of Letters could be associated with the knowledge of saints as well as with "magicians and atheists." Cf. Ibn Arabi, *Le Livre du Mîm, du Wâw et du Nûn*, edited, translated, and presented by Charles-André Gilis, Beirut: Albouraq, 2002.

[8] René Guénon, "The Tree and the *Vajra*" in *Symbols of Sacred Science*, op. cit. Among the titles of the Muhammadan inheritor is *Sahib us-sayf*, the "Owner of the Sword." Shaykh Muhyiddin mentions that it is only for fear of the Mahdi's sword that scholars of the law will choose not to oppose him. Given the earlier description of how each of the Four Gateways has its particular authorities, we may at least understand from this that the sword of the Mahdi is more than corporeal.

[9] When the film was edited still further for television, the screenwriter's name appeared as "Judas Booth," indicating at once Judas Iscariot and the murderer of President Abraham Lincoln,

although Frank Herbert praised Lynch's efforts, he "quibbled" about one matter in particular: "Paul was a man *playing* god, not a god who could make it rain."[10] Despite Herbert's unequivocal attitude, Lynch is not alone in this matter, since his understanding recalls the perspective of *Dune*'s original publisher. For Herbert to accuse Lynch of depicting "a god" is disingenuous; it is rather the "Hand of God," an expression put down by Herbert himself and interpreted by Lynch, who brings rain. Not only is this interpretation in perfect harmony with the symbolism of the *vajra*, it is simply a depiction of what is mentioned in the Traditions concerning the one *"for whom Allah sends rain,"* and so it seems that what Herbert was really quibbling with was a more authentic presentation of his source material.

During his subsequent career, David Lynch would repeatedly explore one story in particular, *Twin Peaks*. Now, this very title recalls the location of the barrier against Gog and Magog, and the story does indeed focus on the intrusion of destructive psychic forces upon the eponymous imaginary town in Washington. The principal character standing against this intrusion - portrayed by the same actor cast as Muad'Dib in *Dune* - is appropriately named Dale Cooper, since a valley or "dale" is a balanced location between mountains, and his efforts are directed at keeping these forces "cooped" up. In the Qur'anic account of the building of the barrier between the twin peaks,[11] Dhul-Qarnayn employs alternatively iron and copper, and traditional commentators relate these materials to the physical and psychic domains. In *Twin Peaks*, the balance of

---

thereby providing a commentary on the betrayal and murder of an artist's vision.

[10] Frank Herbert, *Eye*, New York: ibooks, 2001, page 12.

[11] Qur'an XVIII, 93-8. The enjoinder to "blow" may be understood to relate to the microcosmic attention on the breath, a practice of fundamental importance to Zen Buddhism particularly; and "conscious breathing" is in fact the first of the Eleven Principles of the Naqshbandi way.

these materials finds expression in the secular authority and mysterious way of knowing – depicted as specifically Buddhist – of Cooper; or again, in the "white" authority of the sheriffs Truman (who are obviously "true men")[12] and the "red" heritage of the American Indian Hawk. More obviously, doors between worlds figure in the story, and trees play a prominent role, especially given the town's role in logging, with a log even serving as a mysterious guide.[13]

After the initial run of *Twin Peaks* on television, Lynch directed a feature film "prequel," and completed his story by writing and directing an unprecedented 18-hour "return" to television. What is curious is that *Star Wars*, the chosen stage for George Lucas' artistic efforts, assumed a comparable structure: an initial trilogy, a set of "prequels" directed by Lucas (in apparent fulfillment of Lynch's recommendation), and a "conclusion," albeit without Lucas' involvement and in betrayal of his best efforts.[14] What is more, the prequels in particular focus on Anakin Skywalker, a character who is corrupted by evil, but who

---

[12] At least Sheriff Harry Truman is also a member of the "Bookhouse Boys," a secret fraternal society sworn to defend the town, and its emblem combines the symbols of tree and sword, recalling the conjunction of tree and *vajra*.

[13] The principal door to another world is located at a "Glastonbury Grove." Now, Glastonbury is a real place, of course, the spiritual center of Britain, associated above all with the Grail and Saint Joseph of Arimathea and his staff that became the Glastonbury Thorn. But there are other trees specifically associated with Glastonbury, namely a pair of oaks very curiously called Gog and Magog. In *Twin Peaks*, the curtained room beyond this door obviously stands for the `alam ul-mithal*; and considering the observations made earlier concerning "giants and dwarfs," their roles in this story should not be overlooked.

[14] This "betrayal" of George Lucas following his sale of Lucasfilm might profitably be compared to the betrayal of Lynch's hopes for *Dune*, or even more to the point, the betrayal of *Dune*'s spiritual inspiration - that in turn inspired Lynch - by Frank Herbert himself.

ultimately rejects it and dies in victory; and the *Twin Peaks* prequel focuses in a very similar way on the character of Laura Palmer.[15] Each of these characters might be said to be "between" good and evil, and so they serve to exemplify how balance may not be found through the incorporation of evil.[16] Just as *Star Wars* depicts the Sith opposing balance itself rather than participating in it, *Twin Peaks* concerns an opposition between a Black and a White Lodge that is irreconcilable. Both works are distinguished by an emphasis upon the need to be aligned with truth against the falsehood that parodies it. When the 18-hour work focuses on two rival Coopers, the false Cooper, like the Sith, must ultimately be destroyed.

That is not all. The strange storytelling structure that is shared by *Star Wars* and *Twin Peaks* was actually preceded by the example of *Dune*, since Frank Herbert's original sequence of novels were followed by Brian Herbert's prequels, and concluded with novels set after the original stories. Even stranger, the number of years between the first and last *Star Wars* film, 42,[17] is precisely the span between the publication of *Dune* in 1965 and the concluding novel of 2007. As already indicated, the elaboration of *Dune* confused the image of a dangerous leader claiming legitimacy with the image of Frank Herbert's original inspiration, an expected hero authenticated by the spiritual traditions that Herbert plundered. The reason that this

---

[15] Anakin in the prequels is the "Chosen One;" in *Twin Peaks*, Laura is the "One."

[16] In fact, the name Anakin clearly recalls the giant Anakim noted earlier in relation to Og, and so indicates an "unbalanced form." Good and evil are not complements to be balanced; to imagine otherwise is to accept that either the masculine or the feminine, or the sky or the earth, is equivalent to evil.

[17] This number figures in *Dune* itself, in Book II when Paul-Muad'Dib first joins the Fremen. It also happens to coincide with the title of what is considered the earliest translation into Chinese Buddhism, the *Sutra of Forty-two Chapters*.

confusion should be so problematic is that unlike Lucas' distinct examples of Jedi and Sith, or the two Coopers of *Twin Peaks*, Herbert himself would prove incapable of distinguishing one from the other in his own imagination, or unwilling to do so. Staying true to his vision, when he presented his return of the true Cooper, David Lynch did so with thematic indications that he had Paul-Muad'Dib in mind, and especially the formula that defines his adaptation of *Dune*: "The sleeper must awaken!"[18]

In a real sense, then, both *Star Wars* and *Twin Peaks* were formulated with reference to *Dune*, and they may even be interpreted as manifesting two complementary aspects of Alexander Dhul-Qarnayn. *Twin Peaks* concerns efforts undertaken against unseen forces threatening this world, while the battles of *Star Wars* restore "peace and justice" to the galaxy. The former recalls the more esoteric Qur'anic account, and was made for the more interior setting of television; the latter is a more action-oriented display for the cinema, with its blending of East and West and its lightsabers recalling the legendary conqueror with his sword named Lightning. At the root of both is Usul, the very young conqueror with Greek ancestry, whose story is told in esoteric terms,[19] and who even succeeds in attaining a Water of Life in fulfillment of Alexander's quest.

---

[18] This command is also found in the *Rashahat `ayn al-hayat* concerning an occasional shift from silent to vocal invocations (*dhikr*); this practice has more recently been employed by Shaykh Nazim al-Haqqani and questioned by the narrow-minded. Of course, the use of "the Voice" is a hallmark of the weirding way.

[19] In the best-known Islamic "Book of Alexander," the *Iskandarnameh* of Nizami, the stories of conquest are separated from those of his esoteric pursuits into two volumes. Incidentally, *Dune* as a novel has been adapted for both cinema and television.

8

Golden Gate

Again, the original development of *Dune* occurred in the San Francisco Bay Area of California in the 1960s, and George Lucas' *Star Wars* similarly took shape in the same place in the decades following, at least in part inspired by its predecessor. More generally, the West Coast figures consistently in these matters, and includes the Oregon Dunes as well as Washington state, the location of Herbert's hometown as well as of the imaginary *Twin Peaks*. In *The Red and the White*, the matter of America being a land "in-between" East and West was raised, with special attention given to the West Coast. If a geographic point might be specified as representing this intermediary character, the Bay Area's Golden Gate most certainly qualifies. This designation actually predates the Gold Rush, and was given rather in reference to the Golden Horn of the Bosporus in Constantinople, since East and West may be understood to meet in both places.[1] From the Golden Gate, the twin peaks of Mount Diablo rise in the distance.[2] Marin County lies

---

[1] What is more, both Constantinople and San Francisco are recognized as occupying sites having seven hills, and both are identified by locals simply as "the City," as the modern name of Istanbul (literally, "to the city") made official.

[2] Alfred Kroeber mentions that this sacred mountain "was so named by the Spaniards with reference to the Indian belief in its habitation by spirits" (*Handbook of the Indians of California*, Washington: Smithsonian Institution, 1925, page 472). Apparently, the Spanish believed that its inhabitants belonged to the Underworld rather than the "World of Spirits."

immediately to the north, and once when describing his religious views, Lucas offered, "It's Marin County. We're all Buddhists up here."[3]

West is naturally the direction of sunset, and no doubt America has led the way towards the dark consequences of a materialistic world view. As Shaykh Abd al-Wahid Yahya has established, materialism leads to the breaking down of the cosmic wall, and so it is not by accident that by the end of the 1960s the West Coast should have become a gathering place for the psychoactive drug taking of the "hippies" where openings might be forced in the shell of American life. However, in keeping with the significance of the Golden Gate, there is an eastern aspect to be considered, of no small importance to the hippies. The notion of a Buddhist land in California relates to these developments. The matter of psychedelic drugs in relation to religious experience opens at least a potential awareness of traditional knowledge regarding the latter; Aldous Huxley was the author not only of *The Doors of Perception* but also *The Perennial Philosophy*. In the Bay Area of the 1960s, one of the most influential teachers of Eastern doctrines was Samuel Lewis, who understood his role to be the "spiritual leader of the hippies."[4] It is worth remembering that he claimed to represent traditional lineages not only from Zen Buddhism, but also specifically

---

[3] *Time*, 29 April 2002. The influence of Buddhism rose even to the pinnacle of California politics in the late 20th century, with Jerry Brown devoting himself to Zen Buddhist practices in Japan between his terms as Governor. Again, it was perhaps the "non-theistic" character of Zen that could support and not replace Brown's Christian faith. It may also be worth noting that Brown was educated by the Jesuits, whose name was the inspiration, supposedly, for Herbert's invention of "Gesserit." As for Lucas, he himself has claimed to be "Buddhist Methodist."

[4] Cf. Wali Ali Meyer, "A Sunrise in the West: Hazrat Inayat Khan's Legacy in California," *A Pearl in Wine*, New Lebanon: Omega, 2001, page 425.

the Naqshbandi order of Sufism through Hazrat Inayat Khan, who was also an inheritor of the most celebrated *qalandar* in the history of religion, Lal Shahbaz Qalandar.[5]

In *Return of the Jedi*, Lucas locates his galactic apocalypse among the Redwood trees of California, in the company of the primitive Ewoks whose name serves to recall the Native Miwoks of Lucas' Marin County home. We have mentioned that Herbert had American Indians in mind with his Fremen; Brian Herbert maintains that his father felt closest to the character of the Fremen Stilgar, "the equivalent of a Native American chief in *Dune* – a person who represented and defended time-honored ways that did not harm the ecology of the planet."[6] Indeed, if we recall the warning of Frank Herbert's Native friend concerning "non-Indian civilizations that take and do not give," it will be seen how the balance attained by Usul in relation to "one who gives" and "one who takes" should be understood primarily in relation to this warning. Some would prefer to see the rise of the "off-world prophet" in *Dune* as an expression of white colonial supremacy over Native peoples; but given Herbert's sympathies and the apocalyptic context, we should consider an alternative.

The novel in fact resonates rather profoundly with matters explored in *The Red and the White*.[7] In that work, I pointed out that the traditional American Indian hope for the return of an "ancient white people" was parodied by the historical arrival of invading Europeans.[8] After establishing

---

[5] El-Hajj Malik El-Shabazz, better known as Malcolm X, may be the namesake of this saint. He was martyred in the same year as *Dune*'s publication, 1965.

[6] Afterword to *Dune*.

[7] Among other things, the link between the name "Muad'Dib" and the second moon of Arrakis recalls the particular association of the moon with the "ancient white people" who are the subject of that book.

[8] In *The Secret History of Twin Peaks* (New York: Flatiron Books, 2016), David Lynch's collaborator Mark Frost associates the

House Atreides on Dune, Herbert in his sequels offers an echo of the European invasion of America, when the apparent fulfilment of an expected return brought anything but the hoped-for peace. Nevertheless, the events of the novel itself do indeed deliver a reintegration of traditional ways and a renewal of imperial power, directed by spiritual knowledge, that would give as well as take. As indicated at the conclusion of *The Red and the White*, "California" shares its Arabic root with "caliph," and so it is very revealing that the most influential novel from the psychedelic era in California should so explicitly point to the appearance of the Caliph of God.[9]

The legacy of Frank Herbert's *Dune* is very much "in-between." The novel concerns the rise of the Mahdi; yet Herbert's prediction is unsettlingly accurate concerning the appearance of a false caliphate in the early 21st century. The military conquest of the planetary capital Arrakeen suggests the prophesied conquest of Rome by the Mahdi; yet the implications of using "atomics" against the Shield Wall are sinister.[10] Herbert mines and discovers profound spiritual realities belonging to the "Land of Mountains" lineage of the Naqshbandi Golden Chain in particular, and

---

ancient guardians of Twin Peaks with the "white Indians" who are the subject of *The Red and the White*, chapter 1.

[9] *Star Wars* that follows *Dune* in so many ways might seem to be a departure from this focus on the Mahdi. However, since the emphasis in Lucas' story is remarkably on the spiritual chivalry of Islam (*futuwwah*, literally the "way of youth") as I have long insisted, it must be acknowledged that the Mahdi is traditionally known to be the Seal of Futuwwah. For that matter, the emphasis on the youth of Muad'Dib – and that Stilgar even relates this name to the "instructor-of-boys" – shares in this reality.

[10] The Death Stars of *Star Wars* demonstrate that atomic weapons were a matter of personal concern for Lucas, bringing to mind the role of the Bay Area's Berkeley Lab in their development; and for Lynch's part, *Twin Peaks* presents the intrusion of demonic forces into this world as an immediate consequence of atomic testing.

yet some of its imagery seems to have penetrated the mountainous barrier that is weakening against Gog and Magog.

All this is comprehensible in terms of the `alam ul-mithal. That is the realm where spiritual realities are given form, and so they must exist there before appearing here. At the same time, the World of Images is also where the deceptive shadows of these forms, as it were, originate. Once *Dune* did appear at the determined place and time, it would prove to be much greater than Herbert could have predicted; but its vitality relates to the Water of Life, and so it has challenged the last half century with power that may either destroy or illuminate.

A novelist – or any other artist - may only be expected to have access to this domain of the soul, with all of its confusions. The certainty of the spiritual domain always transcends that realm, and the ignorance of its very existence accounts for darkness in the world. Despite the spiritual source of so much of *Dune*, Herbert did not allow for the `alam ul-arwah, and the conflict between the spiritual certainty of his sources and his own mistrust of this certainty has resulted in confusion concerning Muad'Dib. Just as the appearance of the Antichrist must precede the descent of the Spirit of God, a sort of "anti-caliph" has already appeared in Iraq, suggesting that the Caliph of God must not be far off. Beyond Herbert's art, and beyond his effort to predict, there is this more certain promise pertaining to the descent of the Spirit, and that just as the shadows in *Dune* may have prefigured events in the Middle East, the light of inspiration that shone upon the Golden Gate is reminding the world of the imminence of that descent.[11]

---

[11] The Qur'anic term for spiritual victory in the physical world is from the root *f-t-h*, with the literal meaning of "opening," and this terminology accords with the symbolism of the Four Gateways.

And say: My Lord! Cause me to come in with a firm incoming and to go out with a firm outgoing. And give me from Thy presence a sustaining Power.
And say: Truth hath come and falsehood hath vanished away; Lo! falsehood is ever bound to vanish.[12]

---

[12] Qur'an XVII, 80-81.

www.ingramcontent.com/pod-product-compliance
Lightning Source LLC
Chambersburg PA
CBHW070631050426
42450CB00011B/3158